NIETZSCHE

NIETZSCHE

AS

CRITIC, PHILOSOPHER, POET AND PROPHET

Choice Selections from his Works

COMPILED BY

THOMAS COMMON

I domicile in my own abode;
I would nobody imitate—ne'er;
And—I laugh at every master's mode,
Who to laugh at himself could not bear.

Over Nietzsche's Door.

ROGUE SCHOLAR

First published in 1901

ISBN: 978-1-954357-11-2

Introduction: The Importance of Thomas Common in Early Nietzsche Studies

This anthology was first published in 1901, only a year after Nietzsche had died, and was the first comprehensive selection of his writings to appear in English. The anthologist, Thomas Common, was among the first generation of self-proclaimed Nietzscheans, and the first to devote himself to spreading Nietzsche's ideas in the English-speaking world.

Common was born in 1850 on a farm in Upper Tofts, Roxburghshire, Scotland, where he spent his childhood, never knowing anything of city life until he went off to the University of Edinburgh.[1] He intended to become a Presbyterian minister, as he and his entire family had been converted sometime during his childhood, but during his studies he began to question his religious beliefs, and gave up his plans to enter the Church by the end of his second year in school. Never one to hide his views and opinions no matter how controversial or unpopular, his renunciation of the Christian faith cost him all of his friends at that time.

He went on to study politics and agriculture, but was unclear about what path he should take in life. He left Europe for the Americas, living first in Canada and then the United States. Eventually he returned to Britain,

---

[1] All biographical information on Thomas Common is taken from the memorial written by his sister and published in the final issue of the *The Good European*, the journal which Common had founded and published to promote Nietzsche's ideas.

settling in London so that he could make use of the library and the British Museum to carry out research in philology, to which he was naturally drawn. It was there, sometime in the 1890s, that he discovered the works of Nietzsche. He was seized by them immediately, perhaps seeing something of himself in this son of a Lutheran pastor, once intensely devout but now just as intensely critical and hostile to Christianity.

He read all of Nietzsche's books that he could find and, recognizing their importance, set out to translate them into English. In 1894 he made contact with Nietzsche's publisher in Germany, C.G. Naumann, and made arrangements for authorized English editions of Nietzsche's principal works. He had already begun translating, and had completed *The Case of Wagner* even before reaching an agreement with Naumann. He found other willing translators, such as Alexander Tille, William Haussmann, Johanna Volz and Helen Zimmern (Nietzsche had known Zimmern personally and had suggested her as a translator for his work), and they made plans with a new London publisher, Henry & Co., to publish some of Nietzsche's main works. In 1896 the publisher announced forthcoming translations of *Thus Spake Zarathustra*, *The Case of Wagner* (which included *Twilight of the Idols*, *The Antichrist*, and *Nietzsche Contra Wagner*) *On the Genealogy of Morals*, and *Beyond Good and Evil*.

Common's translation of the Wagner texts and other late works was the first to appear, as volume XI of a projected complete translation of Nietzsche's books which was to be edited and overseen by Tille. This was followed shortly by Tille's translation of *Zarathustra* as volume VIII, and then a year later by Haussmann's translation of *Genealogy* as volume X, which also included a selection of Nietzsche's poems. The books all appeared simultaneously in Britain and in America, where they were published by Macmillan. But the remaining translations never materialized because Henry & Co. went bankrupt and the whole project fell apart.

However, more translations had been made, and they now lingered as unpublished manuscripts. Common never abandoned his role as Nietzsche's apostle in Britain, continuing to write articles about him in the British press defending him from the increasing attacks against him. In 1901 he took the unpublished translations, which apparently included almost all of Nietzsche's books, and created this anthology.[2]

There have been surprisingly few anthologies of Nietzsche, considering that almost all of his books are overflowing with scattershot aphorisms which lend themselves very well to rearranging. Walter Kaufmann's two collections, *Basic Writings of Nietzsche* and *The Portable Nietzsche*, are not really collections of passages but rather of whole books, and while they are an affordable and convenient way to own some of Nietzsche's most important works, they almost wholly omit the *Untimely Meditations*, *Human All-Too Human*, *The Dawn*, and *The Gay Science*—in other words, they pass over Nietzsche's early writings which show a crucial stage in his development and which make the later works, with their seemingly

---

[2] While Common gives thanks and acknowledgment to all of the aforementioned translators in his Introduction to the book, it seems that he only used the translations of others for comparative purposes, such that all translations here are to be considered his.

The original introduction which Common wrote has been omitted from this republication because the biographical information about Nietzsche is widely available elsewhere, and also because much of it is concerned with situating Nietzsche in the context of 19th century Darwinian thought. Common was quite aware of what he called Nietzsche's "Darwinophobia" but, since Darwin and Nietzsche were the two biggest formative influences on him, he retained a lifelong interest in reconciling whatever differences existed between the two. His very last essay, published posthumously in the Memorial edition of *The Good European*, was on Darwin and Nietzsche.

outrageous conclusions and expressions, much more comprehensible and less bombastic. It was not until 1977 that another thematic arrangement of Nietzsche selections appeared in English, that being R.J. Hollingdale's *A Nietzsche Reader*. The more recent *The Nietzsche Reader* from Wiley-Blackwell (*the*, as opposed to Hollingdale's more modest use of the indefinite article) gives a more balanced selection of texts than the Kaufmann volumes but like Kaufmann arranges them chronologically rather than topically.

It is Hollingdale's reader which is the heir to Common's. But while Hollingdale is a fine translator and anthologist, his work dates from the second half of the 20th century, after the great revaluation of Nietzsche enacted principally by Walter Kaufmann, who was Hollingdale's friend and collaborator. This revaluation sought to remove Nietzsche from his association with Nazism and all manner of things which had become politically incorrect in the post-WW2 era. To some extent, all Nietzsche scholarship and commentary since that time has been affected.[3] The present volume, however, does not suffer from this burden, and represents a remarkably fine selection of passages from Nietzsche's work, from *The Birth of Tragedy* all the way up to the final books.

Some of the hostility which Nietzsche's writings encountered in Britain and America at the turn of the century was doubtless because of the unfortunate order

---

[3] Even before World War 2 and Walter Kaufmann, Nietzsche was seen by many as "the prophet of German militarism" and was similarly smeared after World War 1. Before that, he was accused of being a radical anarchist and egoist, since that was the first milieu in America to take up his ideas for themselves. It was and remains Nietzsche's destiny to be chronically misunderstood and misinterpreted—a destiny he was acutely aware of himself.

in which the translations appeared.[4] *Zarathustra* is arguably Nietzsche's most important work, but also his most difficult to understand, wholly different in style from his other books, and much in need of the context of his other writings. *Twilight of the Idols* is an apt and concise summary of Nietzsche's final conclusions about many things, but is a kind of capstone to his entire body of work rather than a stand-alone volume. *The Antichrist* is deliberately polemical and outrageous, while the Wagner texts—although full of a great many insights about art and culture in general, such as the very first selection which appears here—can easily be seen as merely reflecting Nietzsche's falling out with Wagner and thus incidental to his main ideas. Of the first books to be translated into English, only *On the Genealogy of Morals* is a really fitting introductory work, since it is Nietzsche's most systematic and sustained argument. But it was the last of the three to appear after the much-maligned first two, and since the publisher went bankrupt at the same time and was unable to promote the work, it largely fell through the cracks.

A similar fate unfortunately befell *Nietzsche as Critic, Philosopher, Poet and Prophet*. The book had been sponsored by George Bernard Shaw, but its publisher, Grant Richards, went bankrupt soon after its publication. It was therefore neither very successful nor very profitable for Common. It did, however, have some influence in artistic circles. W.B. Yeats read it and was greatly influenced by

[4] In contrast, in France a fairly regular and orderly series of translations were issued by the *Mercure de France*, edited by Henri Albert. Nietzsche had correctly predicted that the French would be more receptive to his ideas than the English.

Nietzsche's ideas—his copy of Common's anthology is filled with notes and underlinings.[5]

Thomas Common continued to champion Nietzsche's ideas for the rest of his life. After the collapse of Henry & Co., he tried in vain to continue the translation of the complete works, a project which came to little because it was first thwarted by Nietzsche's sister and then usurped by Oscar Levy.[6] In 1898 a journal called *The Eagle and the Serpent* appeared, "Dedicated to the Philosophy of Life Enunciated by Nietzsche, Emerson, Stirner, Thoreau and Goethe" all of whom were interpreted through the lens of egoism. Common frequently contributed articles and translations, including portions of his translation of *Zarathustra* as he was working on it. When *The Eagle and the Serpent* ceased publication in 1902, Common founded his own journal called *Notes for Good Europeans*, later changed to *The Good European Point of View*, wherein he continued to write about Nietzsche. He published it intermittently between 1903 and 1916, while also continuing to work on translations. Despite his differences with Oscar Levy and apparent distaste for the man, he contributed his translations of *The Gay Science* and *Thus Spake Zarathustra* to Levy's Collected Works, so

[5] Yeats' annotations are discussed in detail in David Thatcher's *Nietzsche in England* (University of Toronto Press, 1970) p143-152.

[6] According to Common (and borne out by David Thatcher's research), several other publishers were interested in continuing the series, but Nietzsche's sister, who had taken over the publishing rights from Naumann, was not cooperative. The copyright on Nietzsche's works had lapsed, and so, in order to remedy this situation for herself, she set about creating a new "Pocket edition" which combined the published works with unpublished material still under copyright. Rather than work with Common, Tille and the others on the series they had already begun, she ultimately contracted her new edition to Oscar Levy for his Collected Works series some ten years later—which is somewhat ironic since Frau Förster-Nietzsche is reputed to have been a virulent anti-Semite.

that the English-speaking public would be able to read them.

He died in 1919 at age 69, the result of head injuries sustained in a fall. His sister Mary wrote, "If not the first [Nietzschean], he was amongst the first, and his enthusiasm in the cause was unequalled and had in it no taint of commercialism. ... Although undoubtedly he had many bitter moments in connection with what he considered the mismanagement of the Nietzschean cause (a cause dear to his heart and with which his name will ever be associated), yet the latter years of his life were not without enjoyment, for he loved nature in all its varied manifestations and took great pleasure in long walks through the country ..."

As David Thatcher notes, "The value of Common's book lay not in its attitude of prostrate veneration, but in the purpose it served of enabling readers in England to sample Nietzsche's great versatility and range." It is a fine testament to Common's knowledge of Nietzsche's thought, and his dedication to making it more widely known at a time when it had very few proponents.

Rogue Scholar Press
June 2022

CONTENTS

PART I. NIETZSCHE AS CRITIC.

1. Men and their Works.

CONTENTS

3. Ethics.

4. Æsthetics.

5. First and Last Things.

PART III. NIETZSCHE AS POET.

1. Jest, Artifice, and Vengeance.

CONTENTS

NIETZSCHE

Thus Spake Zarathustra, II.

Thus Spake Zarathustra, III.

Thus Spake Zarathustra, IV.

PART I.

NIETZSCHE AS CRITIC.

I. MEN AND THEIR WORKS.

ARTISTS AND PHILOSOPHERS IN GENERAL.

Every art, every philosophy, may be regarded as a medicine and assistance to advancing or decaying life; suffering and sufferers are always presupposed. But there are two kinds of sufferers: on the one hand, those suffering from the *superabundance* of life, who want a Dionysian art, and consequently a tragic insight and outlook; on the other hand, those suffering from the *impoverishment* of life, who seek repose, tranquillity, smooth sea, or perhaps ecstatic convulsion and languor from art and philosophy. They seek actual revenge on life—the most voluptuous kind of ecstasy for such impoverished ones! Wagner meets the double requirement of such persons, just as Schopenhauer does; both of them deny and calumniate life. . . . In respect to artists of every kind, I now make use of this main distinction: has the *hatred* of life, or the *superabundance* of life, become creative in them? In Goethe, for example, the superabundance of life became creative, in Flaubert the hatred of life—Flaubert, a new edition of Pascal, but as an artist with this instinctive verdict in his innermost heart: '*Flaubert est toujours haïssable, l'homme n'est rien, l'œuvre est tout.*' He tortured himself when he composed, just as Pascal tortured himself when he thought—they both felt 'unegoistic.' 'Selflessness'—the *décadence* principle, the desire for the end in art as well as in morals.

'Nietzsche contra Wagner'—'We Antipodes.'

SOCRATES AND EURIPIDES.

Like Plato, Euripides undertook to show to the world the reverse of the instinctive, 'unintelligent' poet; his æsthetic maxim that 'to be beautiful everything must be known,' is parallel to the Socratic principle that 'to be good everything must be known.' We may thus regard Euripides as the poet of æsthetic Socratism. Like himself, Socrates was also a spectator at the theatre, who did not comprehend, and therefore did not appreciate the old tragedy; in alliance with him, Euripides ventured to be the herald of a new artistic activity. If then the old tragedy was destroyed, it follows that æsthetic Socratism was the murderous principle; but in so far as the struggle is directed against the Dionysian element in the old art, we recognise in Socrates the opponent of Dionysus, the new Orpheus who rebels against Dionysus; and although destined to be torn to pieces by the Mænads of the Athenian court, he yet puts to flight the over-powerful God himself, who, as when he fled from Lycurgus, the king of Edoni, sought refuge in the depths of the ocean—namely, in the mystical flood of a secret cult which gradually overspread the earth.

That Socrates stood in close relationship to Euripides in the tendency of his teaching, did not escape the notice of contemporaneous antiquity; the most eloquent expression of this felicitous insight being the tale current in Athens, that Socrates was accustomed to help Euripides in composing. Both names were mentioned in one breath by the adherents of the 'good old time,' whenever it was a question about the popular agitators, to whose influence they attributed the fact that the old 'stalwart' Marathonian capacity of body and soul was more and more being sacrificed to a dubious enlightenment, involving progressive degeneration of the physical and mental powers. It is in this tone, half indignantly and half contemptuously, that Aristophanic comedy is wont to speak of both of them —to the consternation of modern men, who would indeed be willing enough to give up Euripides, but cannot suppress their amazement that Socrates should appear in Aristophanes as the first and head *sophist*, as the mirror and essence of all sophistical tendencies; in connection with which it affords a little comfort to put Aristophanes himself in the pillory, as a rakish, lying Alcibiades of poetry. Without here defending the profound instincts of Aristophanes against such attacks, I shall now indicate, by means of the sentiments of the time, the close connection between Socrates and Euripides. With this purpose in view, it is specially to be remembered that Socrates, as an opponent of tragic art, did not ordinarily patronise tragedy, but only appeared among the spectators when a new play of Euripides was performed. The most noted thing, however, is the close juxtaposition of the two names in the Delphic oracle, which designated Socrates as the wisest of men, but at the same time decided that the second prize in the contest of wisdom was due to Euripides.

Sophocles was designated as the third in this scale of rank; he who could pride himself that, in comparison with Æschylus, he did what was right, and did it, moreover, because he *knew* it was right. It is evidently just the degree of clearness of this *knowledge* which distinguishes these three men in common as the three 'knowing ones' of their age.

The most decisive word, however, for this new and unprecedented esteem of knowledge and insight, was spoken by Socrates when he found that he was the only one who acknowledged to himself that he *knew nothing*; while in his critical pilgrimage through Athens, and calling on the greatest statesmen, orators, poets, and artists, he discovered everywhere the conceit of knowledge. He perceived, to his astonishment, that all these celebrities were without a proper and accurate insight, even with regard to their own callings, and practised them only by instinct. 'Only by instinct': with this phrase we touch upon the heart and core of the Socratic tendency. Socratism condemns therewith existing art, as well as existing ethics; wherever Socratism turns its searching eyes it beholds the lack of insight and the power of illusion; and from this lack it infers the inner perversity and objectionableness of existing conditions. From this point onwards, Socrates believed that he was called upon to correct existence; and with an air of disregard and superiority, as the precursor of an altogether different culture, art, and morality, he enters single-handed into a world, of which, if we reverently touched the hem, we should count it our greatest happiness.

Here is the extraordinary hesitancy which always seizes upon us in presence of Socrates, and again and again invites us to ascertain the sense and purport of this most questionable phenomenon of antiquity. Who is it that ventures single-handed to disown the Greek character, which, as Homer, Pindar, and Æschylus, as Phidias, as Pericles, as Pythia and Dionysus, as the deepest abyss and the highest height, is sure of our wondering admiration? What demoniac power is it which would presume to spill this magic draught in the dust? What demigod is it to whom the chorus of spirits of the noblest of mankind must call out:—

'Woe! Woe!
Thou hast it destroyed,
The beautiful world;
With violent blow,
In ruin 'tis hurled!'

A key to the character of Socrates is presented to us by the surprising phenomenon designated as the 'daimonion' of Socrates. In special circumstances, when his gigantic intellect began to stagger, he got a secure support in the utterances of a divine voice which then spake to him. This voice always *dissuades* him, whenever it comes. In this totally abnormal nature, instinctive wisdom only appears in order occasionally to *oppose* conscious perception. While with all productive men it is instinct which is the creatively affirmative force, consciousness only comporting itself critically and dissuasively; with Socrates it is instinct which becomes critic, it is consciousness which becomes creator—a perfect monstrosity *per defectum*! And we also observe here a monstrous *defectus* of all mystical aptitude, so that Socrates might be designated as the specific *non-mystic*, in whom the logical nature is developed, through a superfœtation, to the same excess as instinctive wisdom is developed in the mystic. On the other hand, however, the logical impulse which appeared in Socrates was absolutely prohibited from turning against itself; in its unchecked flow it manifests a native power such as we meet with, to our shocking surprise, only among the very greatest instinctive forces. He who has experienced even a breath of the divine naïveté and security of the Socratic course of life in the Platonic writings, will also feel that the enormous driving-wheel of logical Socratism is in motion, as it were, *behind* Socrates, and that it must be viewed through Socrates as through a shadow. And that he himself had a boding of this relation is apparent from the dignified earnestness with which he everywhere, and even before his judges, insisted on his divine calling. To refute him here was really as impossible as to approve of his instinct-disintegrating influence. In view of this indissoluble conflict, when he had at last been brought before the forum of the Greek state, there was only one punishment demanded, namely, exile; he might have been sped across the borders as something thoroughly enigmatical, irrubricable and inexplicable, and thus posterity would have been quite unjustified in charging the Athenians with a deed of ignominy. But that the sentence of death, and not mere exile, was pronounced upon him, seems to have been brought about by Socrates himself, with perfect knowledge of the circumstances, and without the natural fear of death: he met his death with the calmness with which, according to the description of Plato, he leaves the symposium at break of day, as the last of the revellers, while the sleepy companions remain behind on the benches and the floor, to dream of Socrates, the true erotic. *The dying Socrates* became the new ideal of the noble Greek youths

—an ideal they had never yet beheld,—and above all, the typical Hellenic youth, Plato, prostrated himself before this scene with all the fervent devotion of his visionary soul.

'The Birth of Tragedy,' §§ 12 and 13.

PLATO.

My distrust of Plato goes deeper than the surface. I find him strayed so far from all the fundamental instincts of the Hellenes, so mis-moralised, so pre-existently Christian (he has already got the concept 'good' as the highest concept), that I should prefer to use the hard expression 'refined cheatery' (or if people like it better, idealism) with reference to the whole phenomenon of Plato, rather than anything else. We have paid dearly for this Athenian going to school with the Egyptians (or with the Jews in Egypt?). In connection with the great calamity of Christianity, Plato is the ambiguity and fascination which made it possible for the nobler minds of antiquity to misunderstand themselves, and thereby enter on the *bridge* which led to the cross. And how much of Plato still remains in the conception of the 'Church,' in the organisation, system, and practice of the Church!

'Twilight of the Idols'—'My Indebtedness to the Ancients,' § 2.

THUCYDIDES.

My recreation, my predilection, my cure for all Platonism has ever been *Thucydides*. Thucydides, and perhaps Machiavelli's *Principe*, are nearest akin to me in their unconditioned determination to impose nothing upon themselves, and in their resolution to see significance in *reality—not* in 'reason,' and still less in 'morality.' There is no better corrective than Thucydides of the pitiable colouring up of the Greeks into an ideal, which the 'classically-trained' youth carries away with him into life as the reward of his public school drilling. One has to turn this historian's writings over line by line, and read his mental reserve as distinctly as his words: there are few thinkers so rich in mental reserve. The *Sophist culture*, I mean the *Realist culture*, attains its most perfect expression in Thucydides; that inestimable movement in the midst of the moral and ideal cheatery of the Socratic schools, which, just then, was breaking out everywhere. Greek philosophy as the *décadence* of Greek instincts; Thucydides, as the great sum, the last revelation of that strong, stern, hard, matter-of-factness, which was instinctive in the older Hellenes. *Courage* in presence of reality distinguishes fundamentally such natures as Thucydides and Plato. Plato is a coward in presence of reality, *consequently* he takes refuge in the ideal; Thucydides is master of *himself*, consequently he also maintains his power over things.

'Twilight of the Idols'—'My Indebtedness to the Ancients,' § 2.

What do I love in Thucydides, why is it that I honour him more than Plato? He has the most ample and impartial delight in everything typical of man and events, and he finds that a quantum of *good understanding* belongs to every type: *this* is what he seeks to discover. He has more of practical justice than Plato; he is not a slanderer and belittler of men who have displeased him, or done harm to him. On the contrary, he sees something great, and something more, in all things and persons, in that he sees types only—what would posterity (to whom he dedicates his work) have to do with what was *not* typical! In him, therefore, as student of human nature, the culture with the *most unprejudiced knowledge of the world*—which had its poet in Sophocles, its statesman in Pericles, its physician in Hippocrates, its physicist in Democritus—attained a last, glorious bloom, the culture which deserves to be named after its teachers, the *Sophists*; but, alas, from the moment of being so named it began all at once to grow pale and intangible to us; for we suspected that it must have been a very immoral culture against which Plato and all the Socratic Schools struggled! The truth is here so intricate and ticklish, that one is reluctant to seize upon it, so the old error (*error veritate simplicior*) may run its old course!

'The Rosy Dawn,' § 168.

CHRIST.

Verily, that Hebrew whom the preachers of slow death honour, died too early; and to many it has proved a calamity that he died too early!

As yet he had known only tears and the melancholy of the Hebrews, and the hatred of the good and just—the Hebrew Jesus; longing for death thereupon overtook him.

Had he but remained in the wilderness, and far away from the good and just! Perhaps he would then have learned to live and love the earth—and laughter likewise!

Believe it, my brethren! He died too early; he himself would have disavowed his doctrine if he had attained my age; he was noble enough to disavow!

But he was still immature.

'Thus Spake Zarathustra' I.—'Voluntary Death.'

PAUL.

Everybody still believes in the dictating of the 'Holy Ghost,' or is under the influence of the after-effect of the belief therein; when a person opens the Bible, it is to 'edify' himself, to find some indication of comfort in his personal trouble, whether important or trivial—in short, he reads into the Bible for his own sake, and reads out of it for a similar reason. That it describes the history of one of the most ambitious and obtrusive souls, and of a mind equally superstitious and crafty, the history of the apostle Paul—who knows anything thereof, except a few scholars? Without this remarkable history, however, without the bewilderments and tempests of such a mind and soul, Christianity would not have existed, and we should hardly have known of a small Jewish sect, whose Master died on the Cross. To be sure, if people had only understood this history at the right time, if they had read, *really read* the writings of Paul, not as the revelations of the 'Holy Ghost,' but with an honest and free spirit of their own, and without thinking thereby of their personal trouble—there were no such readers for a millennium and a half,—it would have been all over with Christianity long ago: as much do these pages of the Jewish Pascal disclose the origin of Christianity, as the pages of the French Pascal disclose its fate and the agency by which it will perish. That the ship of Christianity threw a good part of the Jewish ballast overboard, that it went, and was able to go among the heathen, depends on the history of this one man, a man severely tortured, very pitiable, very unpleasant to himself, as well as to others. He suffered from a fixed idea, or to put it more plainly, from a *fixed*, ever-present, never-reposing *question*: What is the state of the case as regards the Jewish *law*? and especially as regards the *fulfilling thereof*? In his youth he endeavoured himself to give satisfaction to this law, covetous of the highest distinction which the Jews could conceive of—the nation which has cultivated the conception of moral grandeur to a higher degree than any other people, and with whom alone the creation of a holy God, and the notion of sin as transgression of his holiness, have been successful. Paul had become, at the same time, a fanatical defender and guardian of the honour of this God, continually struggling against, and lurking for trangressors and disbelievers, severe and malicious towards them, and inclined to exact the extremest penalties. And now he experienced it in his own heart that a man like him, hot-tempered, sensuous, melancholy, virulent in hatred as he was, *could not* himself fulfil the law; yea, what seemed strangest to him, his extravagant ambition was continually excited to transgress it, and he was *obliged* to yield to this thorn in the flesh. Is it really 'carnal mindedness' which makes him again and again a transgressor? And not rather, as he suspected later on, the law itself behind the 'carnal mindedness,' which must always prove unfulfillable, and allure to trangression with irresistible charm? But he had not then found this way of escape. Many things lay on his conscience—he hints at enmity, murder, sorcery, idolatry, lewdness, drunkenness, and delight in riotous feasting,—and however much he now sought to ease his conscience (and still more his ambition) by the extremest fanaticism in revering and defending the law, there were moments when he said to himself: 'It is all in vain! the torture of the unfulfilled law cannot be vanquished.' Luther may have felt in a similar manner, when in the monastery he sought to become the perfect man of the spiritual ideal; and similarly as with Luther, who one day began to hate the spiritual ideal, the Pope, the saints, and the whole priesthood, with a hatred which was the more deadly the less he was able to avow it—so it happened with Paul. The law was the cross on which he felt himself nailed. How he hated it! What resentment he had against it! How he sought about in order to find some means to *destroy* it—to be relieved for ever from having to fulfil it in his own person. And at last the saving thought flashed upon him, together with a vision, as it was bound to do in the case of an epileptic: to him—the furious zealot of the law. who in his heart was weary to death of it—Christ appeared on a lonely path, with the divine effulgence on his countenance, and Paul heard the words: 'Why persecutest thou *me*?' The essential thing which then happened, however, is that all at once his *mind* became clear. 'It is quite *unreasonable*,' he said to himself, 'to persecute this Christ! Here is undoubtedly the way of escape, here is undoubtedly the perfect revenge, here and nowhere else I assuredly have and hold the *destroyer of the law*!' The patient, sick with the most tormenting pride, feels himself all at once restored, the moral despair is, as it were, swept away, because morality has been swept away, destroyed—that is, *fulfilled*, on the Cross! Hitherto that ignominious death had been regarded by him as the main argument against the 'Messiahship' of which the followers of the new doctrine spoke; but what, if it were *necessary* in order to *do away with* the law! The prodigious consequences of this insight, this wonderful enigma-solving, whirl before his eyes; he becomes all at once the happiest of men; the fate of the Jews, nay, of the whole human race, seems to him to be involved in this insight, in this instant of sudden illumination; he possesses the thought of thoughts, the key of keys, the light of lights: it is around him henceforth that history will revolve! For he is now the teacher of the *destruction of the law*! To die to evil—that is also to die to the law! to live according to the flesh—that is also to live according to the law! To have become one with Christ—that is to have become also the destroyer of the law with him; to be dead with Christ—that is also to be dead to the law! Even if it be still possible to sin, it can no longer be against the law: 'I am beyond the law. If I am now sought to take up the law anew and subject myself to it, I should make Christ accessory to sin'; for the law was there in order that sin might appear—it always made the sin manifest, as strong fluids in the body do in the case of disease. God would never have decreed the death of Christ, if a fulfilment of the law had been at all possible without his death; not only is all guilt now removed, but the essence of guilt itself is destroyed, the law is now dead, the carnal-mindedness in which it resided is now dead—or at least in course of dissolution, corrupting, as it were. Still for a brief period in the midst of this corruption!—that is the lot of the Christian before, having become one with Christ, he rises with Christ, participates in the divine glory with Christ, and becomes a 'Son of God,' like Christ. The ecstasy of Paul is thereby at its height, and likewise the obtrusiveness of his soul. With the thought of becoming one with Christ, all shame, all subordination, all constraint is removed from his soul, and his ungovernable ambition reveals itself as an anticipatory revelling in *divine* glories. This is the *first Christian*, the inventor of the Christian mode of life! Until then there had only been some Jewish sectaries.

'The Rosy Dawn,' § 68.

PONTIUS PILATE.

In the whole of the New Testament only a *single* figure appears which demands our respect —Pilate, the Roman governor. To take a Jewish affair seriously—he cannot be persuaded to do so! A Jew more or less—what does it matter? The noble scorn of a Roman, before whom a shameless misuse of the word 'truth' was carried on, has enriched the New Testament with the sole expression therein *which has value*—which is the criticism and the very *annihilation* of the book: 'What is truth?'

'The Antichrist,' § 46.

THE NEW TESTAMENT.

One does well to put on gloves when reading the New Testament; the proximity of so much impurity almost compels one to do so. . . . I have searched the New Testament in vain for even a single congenial trait; there is nothing in it which could be called free, generous, candid upright. Humanism has not yet made its first beginning here. . . . There are only bad instincts in the New Testament; there is not courage even for these bad instincts. Everything in it is cowardice, shutting-of-the-eyes, and self-deception. All other books become pure when one has once read the New Testament: for example, immediately after Paul, I read with delight the most pleasant and wanton scoffer, Petronius, of whom it might be said what Domenico Boccaccio wrote to the Duke of Parma concerning Cesare Borgia: '*è tutto festo*'—immortally sound, immortally cheerful and excellent.

'The Antichrist,' § 46.

THE 'IMITATIO CHRISTI.'

The 'Imitatio Christi' is one of the books which I cannot hold in my hand without a physiological resistance: it exhales a *parfum* of the eternally feminine, for which one has to be French—or Wagnerian. This saint has such a way of speaking about love that the very Parisiennes become curious about it.—I am told that the *shrewdest* Jesuit, A. Comte, who endeavoured to lead his fellow-Frenchmen to Rome by the *roundabout route* of science, inspired himself by this book. I believe it: 'The religion of the heart.' . . .

'Twilight of the Idols.'—'Roving Expeditions of an Inopportune Philosopher,' § 4.

DANTE.

Dante, or the hyena that *poetises* in the tombs.

Ibid., § 1.

PASCAL.

Christianity has depraved the reason even of the intellectually strongest natures, by teaching men to regard the highest qualities of intelligence as sinful, as misleading, as *temptations.* The most lamentable example is the ruin of Pascal, who believed in the corruption of his reason by original sin, whereas it had only been depraved by Christianity.

'The Antichrist,' § 5.

EUROPEAN BOOKS.

In reading Montaigne, La Rochefoucauld, La Bruyère, Fontenelle (especially the 'Dialogues des Morts'), Vauvenargues and Chamfort, one is nearer to antiquity than with any group of six authors of other nations. In these six authors, *the spirit of the last centuries* of the *old* era has risen anew; taken together, they form an important portion of the great and still continuous chain of the Renaissance. Their books rise above the changes of national taste and philosophical hue, in which books usually glisten at present, and must glisten in order to be celebrated; they contain more real thoughts than all the books of German philosophers taken together: thoughts of the kind which produce thoughts, and which —I am at a loss to complete my definition—it is enough that they seem to me to be authors who have neither written for children nor for visionaries, neither for virgins nor for Christians, neither for Germans nor for—I am again at a loss to bring my list to a close. But to utter a distinct eulogy, they would, if written in Greek, have been understood by the Greeks. On the other hand, how much would even a Plato have been *able* to understand of the writings of our best German thinkers—for example, those of Goethe and Schopenhauer? What would he have thought of the reluctance to keep silent which their mode of writing would have provoked in him? I refer to the defects of obscurity, exaggeration, and occasional leanness, to which the writers in question are least liable among German thinkers, though still far too liable (Goethe, as a thinker, has embraced the cloud more than is proper, and Schopenhauer wanders continually, not with impunity, among the similes of things rather than among the things themselves). On the contrary, what clearness and beautiful definiteness in those French writers! The refined ears of the Greeks would also have been obliged to approve of this art, and one thing they would even have admired and adored—the French wittiness of expression; they *loved* something of the kind exceedingly, without themselves being particularly eminent in that department.

'The Wanderer and his Shadow,' § 214.

GERMAN CLASSICS.

Of the six great patriarchs of German literature, five are unmistakably becoming antiquated, or have become antiquated. . . . I put Goethe on one side: he belongs to a higher species than merely 'national literature'; he therefore does not stand to his own *nation* either in a living, a new, or an antiquated relationship. It is only for the few that he has lived and still lives; for most people, however, he is nothing but a fanfare of conceit, which is blown occasionally across the German frontier. Goethe—not only a good and great man, but a *culture* itself—is an episode without a sequel in the history of the Germans. Who, for example, could have been in any respect comparable to Goethe in the last seventy years of German politics (while, at any rate, something like Schiller, and perhaps even something like Lessing, has been active therein)! But the other five! Klopstock became obsolete in his lifetime in a very respectable manner, and so thoroughly, that the thoughtful book of his latter years, 'The Republic of the Learned,' has never been taken seriously by any one, even to the present day. Herder suffered from the misfortune that his writings were always either new or antiquated; for example, to finer and stronger intellects (like Lichtenberg), even Herder's main work, his 'Ideas for the History of Mankind,' was somewhat antiquated immediately on its appearance. Wieland, who lived profusely, and devoted himself to living, forestalled, like a wise man, the decline of his influence by his death. Lessing still lives, perhaps, but among young, and always younger scholars! Schiller has now passed out of the hands of youths into the hands of boys, all the German boys! In fact, it is a familiar method of becoming obsolete for a book to descend always to more immature stages of growth. And what is it that has pushed aside these five authors so that well-instructed and laborious men no longer read them? It is better taste, better knowledge, higher regard for the true and the actual: consequently, nothing else but the virtues which were first planted anew in Germany by these five authors themselves (and by ten and twenty others of less renown), and now, as a tall forest, spread something of the shadow of oblivion, along with the shadow of veneration, over their graves. But *classics* are not the *planters* of intellectual and literary virtues, but the *consummation* and loftiest luminous peaks thereof, which, being lighter, freer, and purer, still remain when the nations themselves have perished. A higher condition of mankind is possible in which Europe of the nations will be a gloomy oblivion, in which, however, Europe will yet *live* in thirty very old, but never obsolete books—in the classics.

'The Wanderer and his Shadow,' § 125.

FOUR MASTERS OF PROSE.

There have been four very rare and truly poetical men in this century who have attained to the mastership of prose, for which in other respects this century is not suited—owing to its lack of poetry. Not counting Goethe, who is fairly claimed by the century that produced him, I regard only Giacomo Leopardi, Prosper Mérimée, Ralph Waldo Emerson, and Walter Savage Landor, the author of 'Imaginary Conversations,' as worthy of the designation of masters of prose.

'The Gay Science,' § 92.

KANT.

All the philosophers have built their systems under the influence of the seduction of morality, Kant also; their aim, which seemed to be certainty and 'truth,' was really to rear *majestic moral structures*—to use the innocent language of Kant, who designated it as his own, 'not so brilliant, but still not unprofitable' task and work, 'to make the ground level and secure for those majestic moral structures' ('Critique of Pure Reason,' ii. p. 257). Alas! he has not succeeded therewith; on the contrary!—as we must own at the present day. With such an extravagant purpose in view, Kant was just the genuine son of his century (which, more than any other, is entitled to be called the century of extravagance), as fortunately he was also its son in respect to the more valuable side of its character (*e.g.* with the considerable amount of sensualism which he adopted into his theory of knowledge). He also had been bitten by the morality tarantula, Rousseau; the sentiment of moral fanaticism was also at the bottom of his soul, of which another disciple of Rousseau's regarded and acknowledged himself as the executor, namely, Robespierre, ***de fonder sur la terre l'empire de la sagesse, de la justice et de la vertu*** (Speech of 7th June, 1794). On the other hand, no one with such a French fanaticism in his heart could have acted more un-Frenchman-like, more profoundly, more radically, or more German-like—if the word German is still allowable in this sense—than Kant acted: in order to make room for ***his*** 'moral domain,' he saw that it was necessary to posit an undemonstrable world, a logical 'other world'—it was precisely for that purpose that his 'Critique of Pure Reason' was necessary! In other words, ***he would not have needed*** it, unless there had been one thing which he regarded as more important than all—to make the 'moral domain' unassailable, or better still, intangible, by the reason: he felt that the assailability of a moral order of things on the part of the reason was too powerful! For in view of nature and history, in view of the fundamental ***immorality*** of nature and history, Kant, like all good Germans for many ages, was a pessimist; he believed in morality, not because it was proved by nature and history, but in spite of its being constantly contradicted thereby.

'The Rosy Dawn,'—Preface, § 3.

I recollect old Kant in this connection, who, as a punishment for having possessed himself, ***surreptitiously***, of 'the thing in itself'—a very ludicrous affair,—was imposed upon by the categorical imperative, and with it in his heart, ***strayed back*** to 'God, soul, freedom, and immortality,' like a fox which strays back into its cage; and it had been his own force and sagacity which had *broken* open the cage!

'The Gay Science,' § 335.

Among Germans it is immediately understood when I say that philosophy is perverted by theological blood. The Protestant clergyman is the grandfather of German philosophy, Protestantism itself is its *peccatum originale.* Definition of Protestantism: the one-sided paralysis of Christianity—*and* reason. One has only to utter the words 'Tübingen College,' to comprehend what German philosophy really is—*insidious* divinity. The Swabians are the best liars in Germany; they lie innocently. Whence the exultation all over the learned world in Germany (three-fourths of which is composed of the sons of clergymen and teachers) on the appearance of Kant; whence the German conviction, which even still finds its echo, that with Kant a change for the *better* commenced? The theological instinct in German scholars divined *what* was now once more possible. A back-door path to the old ideal now stood open; the conception of a 'true world,' the conception of morality as the *essence* of the world (the two most virulent errors that exist), were again, thanks to a wily, shrewd scepticism, if not demonstrable, at least no longer *refutable.* Reason, the *prerogative* of reason, does not reach so far. . . . The success of Kant is merely a theological success; Kant, like Luther and like Leibnitz, has been an additional drag to the vacillating integrity of purpose of the Germans.

'The Antichrist,' § 10.

POST-KANTIAN PHILOSOPHY.

What is the whole of German Moral Philosophy, from Kant onwards, with all its French, English, and Italian offshoots and accompaniments? A semi-theological attack on Helvétius, a disavowal of the slowly and wearisomely achieved clear glimpses and intimations of the right path, which he had at last suitably delineated and focused. Up to the present day, Helvétius is the most dishonoured of good moralists and good men in Germany.

'The Wanderer and his Shadow,' § 216.

HEGEL.

Hegel was the retarder, *par excellence*, of the victory of scientific atheism, in virtue of his grandiose attempt to persuade us finally of the divinity of existence, by the help of our sixth sense, the historical sense.

'The Gay Science,' § 357.

I believe that there has been no dangerous wavering or crisis of German culture in the present century which has not become more dangerous, owing to the immense and still onward-flowing influence of this Hegelian philosophy. The feeling of being a straggler in the rear of time is certainly paralysing and disconcerting; it must, however, seem frightful and subversive, when, with audacious recoil, such a belief one day deifies this straggler, as the true significance and end of all that has previously taken place—when his conscious wretchedness is put on a par with the consummation of the history of the world. Such a mode of contemplation has accustomed Germans to speak of the 'world-process,' and to justify their own age as the necessary result of this world-process; such a mode of looking at things has raised History, as the exclusively sovereign power, to the place of the other spiritual forces, Art and Religion, under the supposition that it is 'the self-realising notion,' under the supposition that it is 'the dialectic of the spirit of nations,' and 'the final court of appeal of the world.'

This Hegelianly interpreted history has been called sarcastically, the perambulation of God on the earth—a God who, as far as he himself is concerned, is only created by history. This God, however, became transparent and intelligible to himself inside the Hegelian brain-pans, and has already ascended all the dialectically possible stages of his development up to this self-revelation; so that for Hegel, the climax and the goal of the world-process coincided in his own Berlin existence. Indeed, he would logically have been obliged to say that all things coming after him were to be regarded merely as a musical *coda* of this historically important *rondo*, or, more properly, as superfluous. He did not however say so; instead thereof, he implanted in the generations whom he had thoroughly leavened, that admiration of the power of history, which practically veers round every moment into sheer admiration of success, and leads to divine worship of the actual; to express which, one now generally uses the very mythological and excellent German phrase, 'to accommodate oneself to actual facts.' He, however, who has learned to bend the knee and bow the head before 'the power of history,' at last nods his 'Yea' in mechanical Chinese fashion to every power, no matter whether it be government, public opinion, or a majority, and dances exactly to the measure which any 'power' thrums on the strings. If every success contains in itself a rational necessity, if every event is the triumph of the logical, or of the 'idea'—then, just down on the knees at once, and let the whole series of successes be adored!

'The Utility and Harmfulness of History,' § 8.

STRAUSS.

The Philistine as the founder of the religion of the future—that is 'the new belief' in its most impressive form; the Philistine become an enthusiast—that is the unprecedented phenomenon which distinguishes the present time in Germany! . . .

In a roughly comfortable way, Strauss wraps himself up in the shaggy vesture of our ape-genealogists, and extols Darwin as one of the greatest benefactors of mankind, but with shame we perceive that his Ethics are constructed quite independently of the question: 'How do we conceive of the world?' Here was an opportunity to show natural courage; for here he would have had to turn his back on the class he belongs to [the Culture-Philistines], and it would have been necessary for him to have boldly deduced moral precepts for the guidance of life from the *bellum omnium contra omnes* and the prerogative of the strongest—precepts, to be sure, which can originate only in a thoroughly undaunted nature like that of Hobbes, and in an exalted love of truth quite different from that which explodes only in violent invectives against parsons, miracles, and the 'great historical humbug' of the resurrection. For with a genuine Darwinian system of Ethics resolutely wrought out, he would have had the Philistines against him, whom he has on his own side in all such invectives.

'David Strauss, the Confessor and Author,' §§ 4 and 7.

UNIVERSITY PHILOSOPHERS.

Experience teaches us, alas! that in respect to philosophers great by nature, nothing stands so much in the way of rearing and propagating them as the bad philosophers supported by the state. A painful subject, is it not?—of course, the same as that to which Schopenhauer first directed attention in his celebrated treatise on 'University Philosophy.' . . .

The 'freedom' with which the state at present favours some men on behalf of philosophy is really no freedom at all, but an employment which supports the man who holds it. So the advancement of philosophy by the state consists only in the fact that at present it is made possible for at least a number of men to *live* by their philosophy, because they can make a livelihood out of it; while the sages of ancient Greece were not supported by the state, but were, at the most, honoured once on a time, like Zeno, with a golden crown and a monument in the Kerameikos. . . . But no state would ever dare to patronise such men as Plato and Schopenhauer, and misplace them as university professors. Why? Because the state is always afraid of them. . . . And this being the case, it will seek the more to attract to itself philosophers who will pretend that it has philosophy on its side—because it has those men on its side who bear the name of philosophy. . . . Consequently, if any one submits to it to be a philosopher on the part of the state, he must also submit to be so looked upon by the state as if he had waived his claim to follow truth into all its haunts. At least as long as he is patronised and appointed, he must acknowledge something still higher than truth—namely, the state. And not merely the state, but at the same time everything which the state requires for its welfare, for example, an appointed form of religion, the social order, the constitution of the army — above all such things there stands inscribed a *noli me tangere*. Is it possible that a university philosopher can ever have made clear to himself the whole extent of his obligations and restrictions?

I know not; if any one has done so, and still remains an official of the state, he has in any case been a bad friend of truth; if he has never done so—well, I should think that then also he would be no friend of truth..

The learned history of the past [furnished by university philosophers] has never been the business of a true philosopher, neither in India nor in Greece; and a professor of philosophy, when he takes up such work, must submit to it to be spoken of, at best, as a clever philologist, antiquary, linguist, or historian, but never as a philosopher . . . The sole criticism of a philosophy which is possible, and which also proves something—namely, attempting to live according to it, has never been taught in the universities, but always the criticism of words about words. And now, just fancy a youthful mind, without much experience in life, being reserved for the fifty verbal systems and fifty criticisms of them thrown and jumbled together—what dissoluteness, what demoralisation, what mockery of an education for philosophy! In fact, it is even acknowledged that the education is not at all for philosophy, but for a philosophical examination, the notorious and usual result of which is that the examined student—alas! too much examined!—with a sigh, makes the acknowledgment to himself: 'Thank God that I am not a philosopher, but a Christian and citizen of the state!'

What if this sigh were just the purpose of the state, and if the 'education for philosophy' were only an abducement from philosophy? Let us ask ourselves the question. Should it be so, however, there is just one thing to be feared—namely, that the youths will at last find out the purpose for which philosophy is absolutely misused here. The highest thing of all, the production of the philosophical genius, nothing but a pretence? The goal perhaps precisely to hinder the production of this genius? The intention twisted to its very opposite? Well then, alas to the whole intricate policy of the state and its professors!

And can it be that such a thing has already become known? I don't know; at any rate, university philosophy has incurred general neglect and suspicion. This is partly connected with the fact that it is really an inferior race that at present lords it in the professorial chairs; and if Schopenhauer had now to write his treatise on 'University Philosophy,' he would no longer require the club, but would conquer with a bulrush. They are the heirs and posterity of those pseudo-thinkers whom he knocked on the badly perverted heads; they look sufficiently like sucklings and dwarfs to remind one of the Indian proverb: 'According to their deeds, men are born stupid, dumb, deaf and misshapen.' Those fathers deserved such posterity, according to their 'deeds,' as the proverb says. Hence it is beyond all doubt that the academic youths will very soon do without the philosophy which is taught at their universities, and that the non-academic men already do without it. One has only to call to mind one's own student years: to me, for example, the academic philosophers seemed to be men quite apathetic; I looked upon them as persons who stirred up a medley out of the results of the other sciences, who in their leisure hours read newspapers and attended concerts, and who, for the rest, were treated even by their academic associates with a politely masked disregard. One gave them credit for knowing little and for never being at a loss for a mystifying phrase to deceive one with regard to their ignorance. . . . They always found reasons why it was more philosophical to know nothing than to learn something. . . . Their secret impulse was to flee from the sciences and establish a gloomy kingdom in one or other of their gaps and obscurities. . . . Only here and there some of them still soar aloft to an insignificant metaphysic, with the usual results—vertigo, headache, and bleeding at the nose. After they have been so often unsuccessful in soaring among the fogs and clouds, when every instant some rude, hard-headed disciple of the true sciences has been catching at their hind-locks and pulling them down, their countenances have assumed the habitually demure expression and look of persons punished for lying. . . . One cannot even learn logical thinking from them any longer, and in natural estimation of their powers they have discontinued the public disputations which were formerly in use. Undoubtedly on the part of the separate sciences things are carried on more logically, more cautiously, more modestly, and more independently—in short, the procedure there is more philosophical than among the so-called philosophers. . . .

As long as the pseudo-thinkerdom recognised by the state endures, all beneficent influences of true philosophy will be frustrated, or at least hampered. . . . On that account, I call it a requirement of culture to withdraw from philosophy all governmental and academic recognition—to relieve state and academy of the problems incapable of solution by them, of distinguishing between true and spurious philosophy. Let the philosophers grow naturally, deny them every prospect of appointment and incorporation in civic functions, tickle them no longer with salaries, yea, rather persecute them, look unfavourably upon them—ye ought then to see marvels! They will then flee apart and seek a roof anywhere, the poor pretended ones: here a parsonage will open its doors, there a schoolhouse; one will steal in among the staff of a newspaper, another will write manuals for young ladies' schools; the most rational of them will put his hand to the plough, and the vainest of them will go to the court. On a sudden all is empty, the nest is flown; for it is easy to get rid of the bad philosophers—one requires only to withdraw favour from them! And that is in any case more advisable than to patronise publicly any philosophy, be it what it will, on the part of the state. . . .

I know well what objection the state could have made to the whole of these reflections when the beautiful, green Hegelianism grew in all the fields; but since this harvest has been spoilt by the hail [Hagel], and none of the promises about it have been fulfilled, and all the barns remain empty, people would rather not raise further objections, but turn away from philosophy. . . . The state does not any longer require its sanction from philosophy, which has thereby become superfluous for it. . . . Non-academical men have good grounds for a certain general contempt of the universities; they say reproachfully that they are cowardly, that the small ones are afraid of the large ones, and that the large ones are afraid of public opinion; that in none of the questions of higher culture do the universities take the lead, but always limp slow and late in the rear; and that the proper bearing of important sciences is no longer observed. . . . The spirit of the journalist always intrudes more and more into the university, and not unfrequently under the name of philosophy; a polished and glossed delivery, Faust and Nathan the Wise upon the lips, the language and the opinions of our fulsome literary gazettes, indeed recently, gossip about our sacred German music, and even the demand for professorial chairs for Goethe and Schiller—such signs indicate that the spirit of the universities is beginning to confound itself with the spirit of the age. Under the circumstances, it seems to me that it would be of the highest importance if a higher tribunal were created outside the universities, which should also survey and direct these institutions in respect to the culture which they further; and as soon as philosophy withdraws from the universities, and thereby frees itself from all unworthy motives and obscurities, it will necessarily be nothing else but such a tribunal. Without political power, without pay, and without honours, it will know how to perform its duty, free from the spirit of the age, as well as the fear thereof; in short, acting as Schopenhauer lived, as the judge of the so-called culture around him. In that way the philosopher is able to be useful even to the university when he does not amalgamate with it, but surveys it rather at a certain dignified distance.

'Schopenhauer as Educator,' § 8.

GOETHE.

Goethe—no mere German event, but a European product: a grand attempt to surmount the eighteenth century by a return to nature, by an *ascension* to the naturalness of the Renaissance, a sort of self-conquest on the part of the century. He embodied its strongest instincts: its sentimentality, its idolatry of nature, its anti-historical, idealistic, unreal, and revolutionary tendencies. He called to his aid history, natural science, antiquity, Spinoza likewise, and above all, practical activity; he environed himself with strictly defined horizons; he did not sever himself from life, but entered into it; he was not discouraged, but took as much as possible on, in, and upon himself. What he sought was *totality*; he opposed the severance of reason, sensuousness, emotion, and will (preached in the most forbidding scholasticism by Kant, the antipodes of Goethe), he disciplined himself to entirety, he *created* himself. Goethe was a convinced realist in the midst of an age disposed to the unreal: he was affirmative of everything analogous to himself in this respect—he had no more important experience than that *ens realissimum,* named Napoleon. Goethe conceived of a personality, robust and high-cultured, skilful in all physical accomplishments, keeping himself in check, and maintaining his self-reverence; who could venture to allow himself the whole realm and wealth of naturalness, and be strong enough for the freedom; a man of tolerance, not out of weakness but out of strength, because he would know how to use advantageously what would cause the ruin of average natures; a man to whom nothing would any longer be prohibited—unless it were *weakness,*—whether designated virtue or vice. A mind thus *emancipated* stands with a cheerful and confident fatalism in the midst of everything that can happen, in the *belief* that it is only individual things that are reprehensible, that on the whole everything is saved and affirmed—such a mind *no longer denies.*

'Twilight of the Idols'—'Roving Expeditions,' § 49.

CARLYLE.

Carlyle, a man of strong words and attitudes, a rhetorician by *necessity,* who was constantly agitated by the desire for a strong belief *and* the feeling of incapacity for it (in that respect a typical Romanticist!). The desire for a strong belief is *not* evidence of a strong belief, but rather the contrary. . . . A constant, passionate *insincerity* as regards himself—that is his *proprium*; he is interesting, and will remain interesting thereby. To be sure, he is admired precisely on account of his sincerity in England! Well, that is English; and in consideration of the fact that the English are the people of consummate *cant,* it is appropriate enough, and not merely conceivable! At bottom, Carlyle is an English atheist, who seeks a reputation for *not* being so.

Ibid., § 12.

EMERSON.

Much more enlightened, more discursive, more varied, more refined than Carlyle, above all, more happy. One who by instinct feeds exclusively on ambrosia, and lets alone what is indigestible in things. A man of taste, in comparison with Carlyle. Carlyle, who was very fond of Emerson, said of him, notwithstanding: 'He does not give *us* enough to bite at,' which may justly be said, but not to Emerson's prejudice. Emerson possesses the kind-hearted and ingenious cheerfulness which abashes all sternness; he is quite unaware how old he has grown and how young he will still remain; he could say of himself, with an expression of Lope de Vega's: '*Yo me sucedo a mi mismo.*' His mind always finds reasons for being contented and even grateful; and at times he verges on the cheerful transcendence of the worthy, who, returning from a love appointment, *tanquam re bene gesta*, said thankfully: '*Ut desint vires, tamen est laudanda voluptas!*'

Ibid., § 13.

CHAMFORT.

That such a judge of men and of the multitude as Chamfort should have run to the assistance of the multitude, instead of standing apart in philosophical resignation and defence—I am at a loss to explain this fact, except in the following manner:—There was an instinct in him stronger than his wisdom, and it had never been gratified: the hatred of all *noblesse* of blood; perhaps his mother's old and only too explicable hatred, which was consecrated in him by love to her—an instinct of revenge from his boyhood, which waited for the hour to avenge his mother. But then the course of his life, his genius, and alas! most of all, the paternal blood in his veins, had seduced him to rank and co-ordinate himself with the *noblesse*—for many, many years! In the end, however, he could not endure the sight of himself, the 'old man' under the old *régime*, any longer; he got into a violent penitential passion, and *in this condition* he put on the raiment of the mob as *his* special kind of hair shirt! His bad conscience was the neglect of revenge. If Chamfort had then been a little more of the philosopher, the Revolution would not have had its tragic spirit and its sharpest sting; it would have been regarded as a much more stupid affair, and would have had no such seductive influence on men's minds. But the hatred and revenge of Chamfort educated a whole generation, and the most illustrious men passed through his school. Let us but consider that Mirabeau looked up to Chamfort as to his higher and older self, from whom he expected (and endured) impulses, warnings, and condemnations—Mirabeau, who as a man belonged to an entirely different order of greatness, as being the very foremost among the statesman geniuses of yesterday and to-day. Strange that, in spite of such a friend and advocate—indeed, one has Mirabeau's letters to Chamfort,—this wittiest of all moralists has remained unfamiliar to the French, the same as Stendhal, who has perhaps had the most profound eyes and ears of any Frenchman of *this* century. Is it because the latter had really too much of the German and the Englishman in his nature for the Parisians to endure him? While Chamfort, a man with a thorough knowledge of the profundities and secret motives of the soul, gloomy, suffering, glowing—a thinker who found laughter necessary as the remedy of life, and almost gave himself up as lost every day he had not laughed,—seems much more like an Italian, and related by blood to Dante and Leopardi, than like a Frenchman!

'The Gay Science,' § 95.

BEYLE (STENDHAL).

In contradistinction to German inexperience and innocence *in voluptate psychologica* (which is not too remotely associated with the tediousness of German intercourse), and as the most successful expression of genuine French curiosity and inventive talent in the domain of delicate thrill, Henry Beyle may be noted: that remarkable anticipatory and forerunning man, who, with a Napoleonic tempo, traversed *his* Europe, in fact, several centuries of the European soul, as a surveyor and discoverer thereof. It has required two generations to *overtake* him one way or other, to divine long afterward some of the riddles that perplexed and enraptured him—this strange Epicurean and man of interrogation, the last great psychologist of France.

'Beyond Good and Evil,' § 254.

COMTE.

Comte, with his celebrated moral formula, *vivre pour autrui,* has in fact out-Christianed Christianity.

In old age, in accordance with the desire for comfort of all old and tired people, the philosopher seeks to enjoy the results of his thinking, instead of re-examining them and sowing them anew; with that end in view, he has to make these results palatable and enjoyable, and has to remove their dryness, coldness, and insipidness. It thus comes to pass that the old thinker apparently exalts himself above the work of his life, while, in fact, he spoils it, by infusing it with extravagances, sweetening, seasoning, poetical obscurities and mystical lights. It was thus that it befell Plato in the end; it was thus that it befell in the end that great, upright Frenchman, Auguste Comte, whose equal as an embracer and driller of the exact sciences the Germans and the English of this century are unable to furnish.

'The Rosy Dawn,' §§ 132 and 542.

DOSTOIEWSKY.

For the problem of the criminal and those related to him, the testimony of Dostoiewsky is very important—Dostoiewsky, the only psychologist, let me say in passing, from whom I have had anything to learn; he belongs to the happiest chance incidents of my life, still more even than the discovering of Stendhal. This *profound* man, whose depreciation of the superficial Germans has a tenfold justification, perceived that the Siberian convicts, in whose midst he lived for a long time (thoroughly heinous criminals for whom there was no return to society), were quite different from what he expected; in fact, that they were persons carved almost out of the best, hardest, and most valuable material to be found on Russian soil.

'Twilight of the Idols'—'Roving Expeditions,' § 45.

The Gospels present to us precisely the same physiological types which the novels of Dostoiewsky depict.

'The Case of Wagner'—Epilogue.

It is to be regretted that a Dostoiewsky did not live in the neighbourhood of this most interesting *décadent* [Christ]. I mean some one who could have had a proper conception of the thrilling charm of such a mixture of the sublime, the sickly, and the childish.

'The Antichrist,' § 31.

SCHOPENHAUER.

It would be a question whether Schopenhauer, with his Pessimism, *i.e.* the problem of the *worth of existence,* was necessarily only a German? I think not. The event *after* which this problem was to be expected with certainty, so that an astronomer of the soul could have calculated the day and the hour for it—the decline of the belief in the Christian God, the victory of scientific atheism,—was a collective European event in which all races are supposed to have had their share of service and honour. . . . Schopenhauer was the first avowed and inflexible atheist we Germans have had; his hostility to Hegel had its ultimate motive here. The non-divinity of existence was regarded by him as something given, tangible, indiscussible; he always lost his philosophical composure and got into a passion when he saw any one hesitate and make circumlocutions here. It is at this point that his thorough uprightness of character comes in; unconditional, honest atheism is precisely the prerequisite of his raising the problem, as a final and hard-won victory of the European conscience, as the most portentous act of two thousand years' discipline to truth, which in the end no longer tolerates the *lie* of the belief in God. . . . When we have thrust away from us the Christian interpretation of things and condemned its 'significance' as a forgery, we are immediately confronted in a striking manner with the *Schopenhauerian question*: Has existence then a *significance at all?*—the question which will require a couple of centuries even to be completely heard in all its profundity. That which Schopenhauer himself answered with regard to this question was—forgive me for saying so—somewhat premature, somewhat juvenile, only a compromise,—a persistence in and adhesion to the very same Christian-ascetic, moral perspectives, the belief in which had got warning to quit along with the belief in God. But he *raised* the question—as we have said, as a good European, and not as a German.

'The Gay Science,' § 357.

THE FOLLOWERS OF SCHOPENHAUER.

What one sees take place on the contact of civilised peoples with barbarians—namely, that as a rule the lower civilisation first accepts the vices, weaknesses, and excesses of the higher; then, from that point onward, feels the influence of a charm; and finally, by means of the appropriated vices and weakness, also allows something of the valuable influence of the higher culture to leaven it: one can see all this close at hand, and without journeys to barbarian peoples—to be sure, somewhat refined and spiritualised, and not so readily palpable. What are the German followers of *Schopenhauer* still accustomed to accept first of all from their master?—who, in comparison to his superior culture, must seem sufficiently barbarous, to be first of all barbarously fascinated and seduced even by him. Is it his hard, matter-of-fact sense, his inclination to clearness and rationality, which often makes him appear so English, and so unlike the Germans? Or the strength of his intellectual conscience, which *endured* a lifelong contradiction of 'being' and 'willing,' and compelled him also to contradict himself constantly in his writings on almost every point? Or his purity in matters relating to the Church and the Christian God?—for here he was pure as no German philosopher had been previously, so that he lived and died 'as a Voltairean.' Or his immortal doctrines of the intellectuality of intuition, the apriority of the law of causality, the instrumental nature of the intellect, and the non-freedom of the will? No, nothing of this enchants, or is felt as enchanting; but Schopenhauer's embarrassments and shufflings in those passages where the matter-of-fact thinker allowed himself to be seduced and corrupted by the vain impulse to be the unriddler of the world; *e.g.* his undemonstrable doctrine of *one will* ('all causes are merely occasional causes of the phenomenon of the will at this period, at this place,' 'the will to live, whole and undivided, is present in every being, even in the smallest, as perfectly as in all that was, is, and shall be, collectively'); his *denial of the individual* ('all lions are really only one lion,' 'plurality of individuals is an appearance,' as also *development* is only an appearance—he calls the opinion of Lamarck 'an ingenious, absurd error'); his fancy concerning *genius* ('in æsthetic contemplation, the individual is no longer an individual, but pure, will-less, painless, timeless subject of knowledge,' 'the subject, in that it entirely merges in the contemplated object, has become this object itself'); his nonsense about *sympathy* and about the outburst of the *principium individuationis* thus rendered possible, as the source of all morality; including also such assertions as, 'dying is really the design of existence,' 'the possibility does not admit of being absolutely denied *a priori* that a magical effect should not proceed from a person already dead': these, and similar *extravagances* and vices of the philosopher, are always first accepted and made articles of faith; vices and extravagances are, in effect, always easiest to imitate, and do not require a long preliminary practice.

'The Gay Science,' § 99.

WAGNER.

But let us speak of the most celebrated of the living Schopenhauerians, Richard Wagner. It has happened to him, as it has already happened to many an artist: he has made a mistake in the interpretation of the characters he has created, and he has misunderstood the inexpressed philosophy of the art which is especially his own. Richard Wagner had allowed himself to be misled by Hegel till the middle of his life; and he did the same once more, when later on he read Schopenhauer's doctrine between the lines of his characters, and began to express himself with such terms as 'will,' 'genius,' and 'sympathy.' Nevertheless, it will remain true, that nothing is more counter to Schopenhauer's spirit than the essentially Wagnerian element in Wagner's heroes —I mean the innocence of the supremest selfishness, the belief in strong emotion as the good in itself, in a word, the Siegfried trait in the countenances of his heroes. 'All that still smacks more of Spinoza than of me,' Schopenhauer would probably have said. Whatever good reasons, therefore, Wagner might have had to be on the outlook for other philosophers than Schopenhauer, the enchantment to which he has succumbed in respect to this thinker has not only made him blind towards all other philosophers, but even towards science itself; his entire art is more and more inclined to become a pendant and supplement to the Schopenhauerian philosophy, and it always renounces more emphatically the higher ambition to become a pendant and supplement to human knowledge and science. And not only is he allured thereto by the whole mystic pomp of this philosophy (which would also have allured a Cagliostro); the peculiar airs and emotions of the philosopher have all along been seducing him as well! For example, Wagner's excitedness about the corruption of the German language is Schopenhauerian; and if one should commend his imitation in this respect, it is nevertheless not to be denied that Wagner's style itself suffers in no small degree from all the tumours and turgescences, the sight of which made Schopenhauer so furious; and that in respect to German-writing Wagnerians, Wagnery is now beginning to be as dangerous as only some kinds of Hegely have been. Wagner's hatred of the Jews is Schopenhauerian, to whom he is unable to do justice, even in their greatest exploit: the Jews were certainly the inventors of Christianity! The attempt of Wagner to construe Christianity as a seed blown away from Buddhism, and his endeavour to initiate a Buddhistic era in Europe under a temporary approximation to Catholic-Christian formulas and sentiments, are both Schopenhauerian. Wagner's preaching in favour of pity in dealing with animals is Schopenhauerian; Schopenhauer's predecessor here, as is well known, was Voltaire, who already perhaps, like his successor, knew how to disguise his hatred of certain men and things as pity to animals. At least Wagner's hatred of science, which manifests itself in his preaching, has certainly not been communicated by the spirit of charitableness and kindness—nor by the *spirit* at all, as is sufficiently self-evident. Finally, it is of little importance about the philosophy of an artist, provided it is only a supplementary philosophy, and does not do any injury to his art itself. We cannot be sufficiently on our guard against taking a dislike to an artist on account of an occasional, perhaps very unfortunate and presumptuous masquerade; let us not forget that our dear artists are all of them something of actors—they must be so, and it would be difficult for them to hold out in the long run without stage-playing. Let us be loyal to Wagner in that which is *true* and original in him, and especially thereby, that we, his disciples, remain loyal to ourselves in that which is true and original in us. Let us allow him his intellectual humours and spasms, let us, in fairness, rather consider what strange nutriments and necessaries an art like his is *entitled* to, in order to be able to live and grow! It is of no account that he is often wrong as a thinker: rightness and patience are not *his* affair. It is sufficient that his life is right in his own eyes, and carries itself through—the life which calls to each of us: 'Be a man, and do not follow me, but thyself! but thyself!' *Our* life also is meant to carry itself through with our approval! We also are meant to grow and blossom out of ourselves, free and fearless in innocent selfishness! And so, on the contemplation of such a man, these thoughts still ring in my ears to-day, as formerly: 'That passion is better than stoicism and hypocrisy; that to be honourable, even in evil, is better than to subside into traditional morality;

that the free man may be good as well as evil; that the unfree man, however, is a dishonour to Nature, and participates neither in heavenly nor earthly consolation; and finally, that ***whoever would become free must become so by his own efforts,*** that freedom does not fall into anybody's lap as a miraculous gift.' ('Richard Wagner in Bayreuth,' § 11.)

'The Gay Science,' § 99.

HERBERT SPENCER.

It follows from the laws of class distinction, that the learned, in so far as they belong to the intellectual middle class, are prevented from getting a sight of the really ***great*** problems and interrogative signs; besides, their outlook, just like their courage, does not reach so far; and, above all, their need which makes them investigators, their innate anticipating and wishing that things may be constituted so-and-so, their fearing and hoping are set at rest and quieted too quickly. For example, that which makes the pedantic Englishman, Herbert Spencer, so enthusiastic in his way, and impels him to draw a cheering streak, an horizon line of desirability, the final reconciliation of 'egoism and altruism' of which he talks—that almost causes nausea to people like me. An humanity with such Spencerian perspectives as ultimate perspectives would seem to us deserving of contempt, of extermination! But the fact that something has to be taken by him as his highest hope, which is regarded, and can be regarded by others merely as a repulsive possibility, is an interrogative sign which Spencer could not have foreseen.

'Joyful Science,' § 373.

My objection to the whole of the sociology of England and France is that it only knows *decaying types* of society by experience, and quite innocently takes its own instincts of decay as the standard for sociological valuations. *Deteriorating* life, the decline of all organising power (*i.e.* separating, gap-making, subordinating, and superordinating power), is formulated as the *ideal* in the sociology of the present day. Our Socialists are *décadents*; Mr. Herbert Spencer, however, is also a *décadent*—he sees something desirable in the triumph of altruism.

'Twilight of the Idols'—'Roving Expeditions,' § 37.

All purpose, all usefulness, is merely a sign that a will to power has got the upper-hand of something less powerful, and has impressed upon it the significance of a function; and the whole history of a 'thing,' of an organ, of a usage, may thus be a continued chain of signs, with ever new interpretations and arrangements. . . . I give prominence to this principal standpoint of historical method, the more so as it runs diametrically counter to the prevailing instinct and taste of the age, which would rather content itself with absolute chance, yea, with the mechanical senselessness of all that happens, than with the theory of a *Will to Power* operating everywhere. The democratic idiosyncrasy towards all that rules and wants to rule, the modern *misarchism* (to coin a bad word for a bad thing) has gradually so transformed and masked itself in the intellectual, the most intellectual guise, that it at present presses, and is *allowed* to press step by step into the exactest and most objective sciences; indeed, it appears to me to have already gained the ascendency over the whole of physiology and the theory of life, obviously to their injury, since it has juggled them out of a fundamental conception, that of the real *activity*. Instead thereof, 'adaptation' is put in the foreground, an activity of secondary rank, a mere re-activity; indeed, life itself has been defined as the more and more suitable internal adjustment to external conditions (Herbert Spencer). The essence of life, however, its *Will to Power*, is thereby misunderstood; its main pre-eminence, which the spontaneous, aggressive, encroaching, new-interpreting, new-directing and moulding forces involve (on the operation of which 'adaptation' results), is thereby overlooked; the commanding *rôle* of the highest functionaries in which the life-will of the organism manifests itself actively and formatively is thereby denied. One recollects what Huxley has reproached Spencer for—his 'administrative Nihilism'; it is a question, however, about *more* than 'administration.'

'Genealogy of Morals,' ii. 12.

NIETZSCHE ON HIMSELF.

It is no pride that has sealed my lips so long, but rather the humility of a sufferer who is ashamed to betray how much he suffers. An animal when it is sick creeps away into a dark cellar, and so likewise does the *bête philosophe*. . . . I am alone, absurdly alone, and in my unflinching and arduous struggle against all that men have hitherto valued and reverenced, I have become a sort of dark cellar myself . . . something hidden and mysterious, that is not to be found even when it is sought. . . . Yet between you and me, it is not impossible that I am the greatest philosopher of the century, perhaps even more than that. I am a decisive and fateful link between two thousand centuries.

Letter to Baron von Seydlitz in 1888.

II. NATIONS AND THEIR CULTURES.

EUROPE IN GENERAL.

Our present-day Europe, the scene of a precipitate, senseless attempt to blend thoroughly both classes and races, is therefore sceptical in all the heights and depths of its being; sometimes with the nimble scepticism which springs impatiently and wantonly from branch to branch; sometimes gloomily, like a cloud overcharged with interrogative signs;—and often sick unto death of its will! Paralysis of the will: where does one fail to find this cripple sitting at present? And yet how bedecked often! How seductively decked out! There are the finest parade dresses and disguises for this disease; and that, for example, most of what is at present exhibited in the show-cases as 'objectivity,' 'the scientific spirit,' '*l'art pour l'art*,' 'pure, voluntary, knowing,' etc., is merely decked-out scepticism and paralysis of will.—I will answer for this diagnosis of the European disease.—The disease of the will is diffused unequally over Europe: it shows itself most extensively and multifariously where civilisation has longest been indigenous, it decreases in proportion as 'the barbarian' still—or again—asserts his rights under the loose robe of western culture. . . . The power to exercise will, and the prolonged power also, is somewhat stronger in Germany than in France; and in North Germany again, it is stronger than in Middle Germany. It is considerably stronger in England, Spain, and Corsica, associated with phlegm in the former, and with the hard skull in the latter.

'Beyond Good and Evil,' § 208.

RUSSIA.

Russia, the only power at present which has durability in its constitution, which can wait, and can yet promise something—the antithetical conception to the pitiable, European, petty-state system, which has got into a critical condition with the establishment of the German empire.

'Twilight of the Idols'—'Roving Expeditions,' § 39.

The power to exercise will is strongest of all and most astonishing in that immense intermediate empire where Europe seems to flow back to Asia—namely, in Russia. There, this power has for long been continuously hoarded and stored up; there, the will—uncertain whether to be negative or affirmative—waits threateningly to be *discharged* (to borrow their favourite expression from our physicists). Probably not only Indian wars and complications in Asia would be necessary in order that Europe might be relieved from its greatest danger, but also internal subversion, the shattering of the empire into small states, and above all the introduction therein of parliamentary imbecility, together with the obligation of everybody to read his newspaper at breakfast. I say this not as one desiring it; the reverse would rather be in accordance with my sentiments—I mean such an augmentation of the threateningness of Russia that Europe would have to resolve to be equally threatening; that is to say, it would have to *acquire one will*, by the institution of a new caste to rule over the country, a persistent, dreadful, spontaneous will, which can set itself goals to be attained millenniums hence—so that the long-spun comedy of its petty-state system, and its dynastic as well as democratic multi-volitionism may finally come to an end. The time for petty politics is past: the next century will bring the struggle for the dominion of the earth—the *necessity* for grand politics.

'Beyond Good and Evil,' § 208.

GERMANY.

A foreigner who travelled in Germany gave dissatisfaction and satisfaction by some of his observations, according to the districts in which he stayed. All Swabians who have intellect—he was accustomed to say—are coquettish.—The other Swabians, however, have always thought that Uhland was a poet, and that Goethe was immoral.—The best thing in the famous German novels at present is that one does not need to read them, one knows them already.—The Berliner appears to be more good-natured than the South German, because he is far too fond of bantering, and on that account endures bantering, which is not encountered by the South German.—The intellect of Germans is kept down by their beer and their newspapers; he would recommend to them tea and pamphlets for curing these evils naturally.—Let us look at the different nations of the now aged Europe, he suggested, with respect to how each of them exhibits particularly well some definite characteristic of age, to the delight of those who sit in front of this stage: how happily the French represent the prudent and amiable aspects of age; the English, its experience and reservedness; the Italians, its innocence and unprejudicedness. Can the other marks of age, then, be lacking? Where is the haughty old man? the tyrannical old man? the covetous old man?—The most dangerous part of Germany is Saxony and Thuringia: nowhere has there been greater intellectual activity and knowledge of human nature, along with freedom of spirit; and all is so modestly concealed by the uncouth language and eager officiousness of this population that it would hardly be remarked that here one has to do with the intellectual sergeant-majors of Germany and its teachers in good and bad.—The insolence of North Germans is kept within bounds by their tendency to obey, that of

South Germans by their inclination to make themselves comfortable.—It appeared to him that the German men had unhandy, though very self-confident housekeepers in their wives; they spoke favourably of themselves so persistently, that they had almost convinced the world, and at all events their husbands, of the specially German housewife-virtues.—If the conversation then turned to Germany's politics, home and foreign, he was accustomed to relate—he called it betray—that Germany's greatest statesman did not believe in great statesmen.—He found the future of the Germans threatened and threatening; for they had forgotten how to *rejoice* (which the Italians understood so well), and owing to the great hazard game of wars and dynastic revolutions, they had *accustomed themselves to emotion*; consequently, they would have an *émeute* some day. For that is the strongest emotion a nation can obtain.—The German Socialist is just on that account the most dangerous, because no *definite* need impels him; his suffering is not to know what he wants; so whenever he attains to anything considerable, he will still languish with covetousness even in the enjoyment, just like Faust, but presumably like a very proletarian Faust. 'The *Faust-devil*,' he exclaimed in conclusion, 'by which cultured Germans were so much tormented, has been driven out of them by Bismarck; now, however, the devil has gone into the swine, and worse than at any previous time.'

'Miscellaneous Opinions and Apophthegms,' § 324.

When the Germans began to become interesting to the other nations of Europe—it is not too long ago,—it took place owing to a culture which they now no longer possess, which in fact they have shaken off with passionate eagerness, as if it had been a disease; and yet they have known of nothing better to exchange for it than political and national insanity. To be sure, they have thereby attained the distinction of having become far more interesting to the other nations than they formerly were on account of their culture, and they may thus have their satisfaction! Meanwhile it cannot be denied that German culture has befooled Europeans, and that it was not worth such interest, yea, such imitation and emulous appropriation as was bestowed on it. Let us just look around to-day at Schiller, William von Humboldt, Schleiermacher, Hegel and Schelling, let us read their correspondence and introduce ourselves into the great circle of their followers: what is it that is common to them all, what is it in them that operates upon us, as we are at present, so unbearably on the one hand, and so movingly and pitiably on the other? In the first place, there is the mania for appearing, at all costs, to be morally *provoked*; then, there is the desire for brilliant, unsubstantial generalities, together with the determination to have a more beautiful view with regard to everything (characters, passions, times, morals)—alas, 'beautiful' according to a bad, undistinguishing taste, which nevertheless boasted of its Greek origin. It is a tender, good-natured, silvery-glistening idealism, which above all wants to have nobly disguised attitudes and nobly disguised voices; a thing as assuming as it is innocent,—inspired by a cordial antipathy to 'cold' or 'dry' actuality, to anatomy, to copious emotions, to every kind of philosophical abstinence and scepticism, but especially to the knowledge of nature which cannot be used as religious symbolism. Of this procedure of German culture, Goethe was a spectator in his usual way: standing by, gently resisting it, silent, and always fortifying his resolution to pursue his own better course. Schopenhauer was also a spectator of it somewhat later,—to him, much of the actual world, and devilry of the world, had again become visible, and he spoke thereof with as much bluntness as enthusiasm; for this devilry has its *beauty*!—And what was it, at bottom, which seduced the foreigners, so that they could neither view this movement as Goethe and Schopenhauer, nor simply look away therefrom? It was the dim lustre, the enigmatical Milky-way light which shone around this culture. The foreigners thereupon said to themselves: 'That is very, very remote from us; our seeing, hearing, understanding, enjoying and estimating are all at a loss there; nevertheless it might be stars! Can it be that the Germans have quietly discovered a corner of the heavens, and located themselves there? One must endeavour to approach nearer to the Germans.' And they came nearer to the Germans; while very little later the same Germans began to be anxious to divest themselves of the Milky-way lustre; they knew so well that they had not been in heaven—but in a cloud!

'The Rosy Dawn,' § 190.

FRANCE.

One cannot call it in question that the French have been the *most Christian* nation in the world, not in respect to the faith of the masses having been greater in France than elsewhere, but because the Christian ideals most difficult of realisation have there incarnated themselves in flesh and blood, and have not remained merely ideas, professions, or partial realisations. There is Pascal, the first of all Christians, by his combination of fervour, intelligence, and integrity—one may well consider what elements had to combine in his case! There is Fénelon, the most perfect and seductive expression of *ecclesiastical culture* in all its powers: a golden mean, which historically one might consider an impossibility, while it has only been something unspeakably difficult and improbable. There is Madame de Guyon, among her equals, the French Quietists: and everything which the eloquence and ardour of the apostle Paul has endeavoured to disclose regarding the most sublime, loving, serene, ecstatic semi-divinity of the Christian has there become realised, while it has divested itself of the Jewish obtrusiveness with respect to God, characteristic of Paul,—owing to the genuine, womanly, refined, noble, Old-French naïveté in language and demeanour. There is the founder of the Trappist monasteries, the last person who took the ascetic ideal of Christianity seriously, not as an exception among the French; but as genuinely French; for up to the present his sombre organisation has only been capable of being indigenous and powerful among the French, it has followed them into Alsace and to Algeria. Let us not forget the Huguenots: the combination of the martial and industrial spirit, of refined manners and Christian austerity, has never yet been more finely exhibited than among them. And at Port Royal, profound Christian erudition blossomed forth for the last time: and the great men of France understand this blossoming better than elsewhere. Far from being superficial, a great Frenchman has always his surface, the natural epidermis of his content and depth; while the depth of a great German is for the most part kept, as it were, under lock and key in an intricately formed case, like an elixir meant to be protected from light and from wanton hands in a hard and curious alembic. And now we can guess why it is that this nation of the most perfect types of Christianity must also produce the most perfect countertypes of the un-Christian free-spirit! The French free-spirit has always struggled inwardly against great men, and not only against dogmas and sublime abortions, like the free spirits of other nations.

'The Rosy Dawn,' § 192.

It is in France of the present day, as can be disclosed and comprehended with equal readiness, that the will is most infirm; and France, which has always had a masterly skilfulness in converting even the most portentous crises of its spirit into the charming and seductive, shows most appropriately its intellectual preponderance over Europe, by being the school and exhibition of all the enchantment of scepticism.

'Beyond Good and Evil,' § 208.

Even at present, France is still the seat of the most intellectual and refined culture of Europe, it is still the high school of taste; but one must know how to find this 'France of taste.' Those who belong to it keep themselves well concealed: there may be a small number in whom it lives and is embodied, besides perhaps being men who do not stand upon the strongest legs, in part fatalists, hypochondriacs, invalids, in part persons over-indulged, over-refined, such as have the *ambition* to conceal themselves. They have all something in common: they keep their ears closed in presence of the delirious folly and noisy spouting of the democratic *bourgeois*. In fact, a besotted and brutalised France at present sprawls in the foreground—it recently celebrated a veritable orgy of bad taste, and at the same time of self-admiration, at the funeral of Victor Hugo. There is also something else common to them: a good predilection to resist intellectual Germanising—and a still better inability to do so! In this France of intellect, which is also a France of pessimism, Schopenhauer has perhaps become more at home and more indigenous than he has ever been in Germany; not to speak of Heinrich Heine, who has long ago been reincarnated in the more refined and fastidious lyrists of Paris; or of Hegel, who at present, in the person of Taine—the *first* of living historians—exercises an almost tyrannical influence. As regards Richard Wagner, however, the more French music learns to adapt itself to the actual needs of the *âme moderne*, the more will it 'Wagnerize'; one can safely predict that beforehand—it is already taking place sufficiently.

There are, however, three things which the French can still boast of with pride as their heritage and possession, and as indelible tokens of their ancient intellectual superiority in Europe, in spite of all voluntary or involuntary Germanising and vulgarising of taste. *Firstly*, the capacity of artistic emotion, of devotion to 'form,' for which the expression, *l'art pour l'art*, along with a thousand others, has been invented; such capacity has not been lacking in France for three centuries, and owing to its reverence for the 'cultured few,' it has again and again made a sort of chamber-music of literature possible, which is sought for in vain elsewhere in Europe. The *second* thing whereby the French can lay claim to a superiority over Europe is their ancient, many-sided, *moralistic* culture, owing to which one finds on an average even in the petty *romanciers* of the newspapers and chance *boulevardiers de Paris* a psychological sensitiveness and curiosity, of which, for example, one has no conception (to say nothing of the thing itself!) in Germany. The Germans lack a couple of centuries of the moralistic work requisite thereto, which, as we have said, France has not grudged: those who call the Germans 'naïve' on that account give them commendation for a defect. . . . They have yet a *third* claim to superiority: in the French character, there is a successful half-way synthesis of the north and south, which makes them comprehend many things and enjoins upon them other things which an Englishman can never comprehend. Their temperament, turned alternately to and from the south, in which from time to time the Provençal and Ligurian blood froths over, preserves them from the dreadful, northern grey-in-grey, from sunless conceptual-spectres and from poverty of blood—our *German* infirmity of taste, for the excessive prevalence of which at the present moment, blood and iron, I mean 'high politics,' has with great resolution been prescribed (according to a dangerous empiricism which bids me wait and wait, but not yet hope). There is also still in France a favourable preunderstanding and ready welcome for the more rare and rarely gratified men, who are too ample to find satisfaction in any kind of fatherlandism, and in the north love the south, and in the south the north—the born Mediterranean men, the 'good Europeans.'—It is for them that *Bizet* has made music, the last genius who has seen a new beauty and seduction —who has discovered a piece of the *musical south.*

'Beyond Good and Evil,' § 254.

ENGLAND.

I see no one in Europe who has (or *discloses*) an idea of the fact that philosophising concerning morals might be conducted in a dangerous, captious, and ensnaring manner—that *calamity* might be involved therein. Observe, for example, the indefatigable, inevitable English Utilitarians: how ponderously and respectably they stalk on and stalk along in the footsteps of Bentham, just as he had already stalked in the footsteps of the respectable Helvétius (no! he was not a dangerous man, Helvétius, *ce sénateur Pococurante,* as Galiani said). No new thought, nothing of the nature of a finer turning or better expression of an old thought, not even a proper history of what has been previously thought on the subject: an *impossible* literature, taking it all in all, unless one knows how to leaven it with some mischief. Of course, the old English vice called *cant,* which is in fact *moral Tartuffism,* has insinuated itself also into these moralists (whom one must read with an eye to their motives, if one *must* read at all), concealed this time under the new form of the scientific spirit; moreover, there is not absent from them a secret struggle with the pangs of conscience, from which a race of former Puritans must very naturally suffer, in all their scientific tinkering with morals. (Is not a moralist the opposite of a Puritan? That is to say, as a thinker who regards morality as questionable, as worthy of investigation, in short, as a problem? Is moralising not—immoral?) In the end, they all want *English* morality to be recognised as authoritative, inasmuch as mankind, or the 'general utility,' or 'the happiness of the greatest number—' no! the happiness of *England* will be best served thereby. They would like, by all means, to convince themselves that the striving after *English* happiness, I mean after *comfort* and *fashion* (and in the highest instance a seat in Parliament), is at the same time the true path of virtue; in fact, that in so far as there has been virtue in the world hitherto, it has just consisted in such striving. Not one of those ponderous, conscience-stricken herding animals (who undertake to advocate the cause of egoism as conducive to the general welfare), wants to have any knowledge or inkling of the facts that the 'general welfare' is no ideal, no goal, no notion that can be at all grasped, but is only a nostrum—that what is fair to one *cannot* at all be fair to another, that the requirement of one morality for all is really a detriment to higher men, in short, that there is a *distinction of rank* between man and man, and consequently, also, between morality and morality.

'Beyond Good and Evil,' § 228.

They are not a philosophical race—the English: Bacon represents an *attack* on the philosophical spirit generally, Hobbes, Hume, and Locke, a debasement and depreciation of the idea of a 'philosopher' for more than a century. It was *against* Hume that Kant rebelled and rose up; it it was Locke of whom Schelling could say: '*Je méprise Locke*'; in the struggle against the English mechanical stultifying of the world, Hegel and Schopenhauer (along with Goethe) were of one accord, the two hostile brother-geniuses in philosophy, who pushed in different directions towards the antithetical poles of German thought, and thereby did injustice to one another, as only brothers can do. . . .

It is characteristic of such an unphilosophical race as the English to hold on firmly to Christianity; they *need* its discipline for 'moralising' and humanising. The Englishman, more gloomy, sensual, headstrong, and brutal than the German, is for that very reason, as the baser of the two, also the most pious.; he has all the *more need* of Christianity. To finer nostrils, this English Christianity itself has still a characteristic English taint of spleen and alcoholic excess, for which, owing to good reasons, it is used as an antidote—the finer poison to neutralise the coarser; a finer form of poisoning is in fact a step in advance with coarse-grained people, a step towards spiritualisation. The English coarseness and rustic demureness is still more satisfactorily disguised by Christian pantomime, and by praying and psalm-singing (or, more correctly, it is thereby explained and differently expressed); and for the herd of drunkards and rakes who formerly learned moral grunting under the influence of Methodism (and more recently as the 'Salvation Army'), a penitential fit may really be the relatively highest manifestation of 'humanity' to which they can be elevated: so much may reasonably be admitted.

'Beyond Good and Evil,' § 252.

Finally, let it be borne in mind that the English, with their profound mediocrity, brought about, once before, a general depression of European intelligence. What is called 'modern ideas,' or 'the ideas of the eighteenth century,' or 'French ideas' —that consequently against which the *German* mind rose with the profoundest disgust—is of English origin, there is no doubt about it. The French were only the apes and actors of these ideas, their best soldiers, and likewise, alas! their first and thoroughest *victims*; for owing to the diabolical Anglomania of 'modern ideas,' the *âme française* has in the end become so thin and emaciated, that at present one recalls its sixteenth and seventeenth centuries, its profound, passionate strength, its inventive excellency, almost with disbelief. One must, however, maintain the verdict of historical justice in a determined manner, and defend it against present prejudices and appearances. The European *noblesse*—of sentiment, taste and manners, taking the word in every high sense—is the work and invention of *France*; the European ignobleness, the plebeianism of modern ideas, is *England's* work and invention.

'Beyond Good and Evil,' § 253.

PART II.

NIETZSCHE AS PHILOSOPHER.

I. GENERAL ATTITUDE.

WE HOMELESS ONES—THE GOOD EUROPEANS.

Among the Europeans of to-day there are not lacking those who may call themselves, in a contrasting and honouring sense, homeless ones; it is precisely by them that my secret wisdom and *gaya scienza* is to be laid to heart. For their lot is hard, their hope uncertain; it is an artifice to devise consolation for them. But what does it matter! We children of the future, how *could* we be at home in the present? We are unfavourable to all ideals which would make us feel at home in this frail, broken-down, transition period; and as regards the 'realities' thereof, we do not believe in their *endurance*. The ice which still carries has become very thin; the thawing wind blows; we ourselves, we homeless ones, help to break the ice, and the other too thin 'realities.' We 'conserve' nothing, nor would we return to any past age; we are not at all 'liberal,' we do not labour for 'progress,' we do not need first to stop our ears to the song of the market-place sirens of the future—what they sing: 'equal rights,' 'free society,' 'no longer either lords or slaves,' does not allure us!—we do not by any means think it desirable that the kingdom of righteousness and peace should be established on earth (because under any circumstances it would be the kingdom of the profoundest mediocrity and Chinaism); we rejoice in everything which, like ourselves, loves danger, war and adventure, which does not make compromises, nor let itself be captured, conciliated, or defaced; we count ourselves among the conquerors; we ponder over the need of a new order of things, even of a new slavery—for the strengthening and elevation of the type 'man' always involves a new form of slavery. Is it not obvious that with all this we must feel ill at ease in an age which claims the honour of being the most humane, gentle, and just on which the sun has shone? It is bad enough, is not it, that precisely in connection with these fine words our innermost thoughts are the more unpleasant; that we see therein only the expression—or even the masquerade—of profound weakening, exhaustion, age, and declining power? What does it matter to us with what kind of tinsel a sick person decks out his weakness! He may parade it as his *virtue*; there is certainly no doubt that weakness makes people gentle, ah, so gentle, so just, so inoffensive, so 'humane'!—The 'religion of sympathy' to which people would like to persuade us—yes, we know the hysterical mannikin and girl sufficiently well who need precisely this religion at present for a cloak and adornment!

We are no humanitarians; we should not dare to speak of our 'love to mankind'; for that, a person of our stamp is not enough of a stage-player! Or not sufficiently Saint-Simonist, not sufficiently French? A person must have been affected with a *Gallic* excess of erotic susceptibility and amorous impatience even to approach mankind with his ardour in an honourable manner. Mankind! Was there ever a more hideous old woman among all the old women (unless perhaps it were 'the truth': a question for philosophers)? No, we do not love mankind! Nor, on the other hand, are we nearly German enough (in the sense in which the word 'German' is current at present) to advocate nationalism and race-hatred, or take delight in the national heart-itch and blood-poisoning, on account of which the nations in Europe are at present bounded off and secluded from one another as by quarantines. We are too unprejudiced for that, too perverse, too fastidious; also too well informed, too much 'travelled.' We prefer much rather to live on mountains, apart, 'unseasonable,' in past or coming centuries, in order merely to spare ourselves the silent rage to which we know we should be condemned as witnesses of politics which make the German nation barren by making it vain, and which are *petty* politics besides. . . . We homeless ones are too divers and mixed as regards race and descent to be 'modern men.' . . . We are, in a word—and it shall be our word of honour!—*good Europeans,* the heirs of Europe, the rich, over-wealthy heirs, also the too greatly obligated heirs, of millenniums of European thought; as such we have also outgrown Christianity, and are disinclined to it—and precisely because we have *sprung from it,* because our forefathers were Christians uncompromising in their Christian integrity, who willingly sacrificed possessions and positions, blood and fatherland, for the sake of their belief. We—do the same? For what, then? For our unbelief? For all sorts of unbelief? Nay, ye know better than that, my friends! The hidden Yea in you is stronger than all the Nays and Perhapses, of which you and your age are sick; and when ye are obliged to put out to sea, ye emigrants, it is—a belief which forces you also thereto.

'The Gay Science,' § 377.

OUR CONSCIENCE.

But there is no doubt about it; there is still a 'thou shalt' which speaks to us, we still render obedience to a strict supreme law. And this is the ultimate morality which still makes itself audible to us, which even we know to be still *living*; here, if in anything, we also are still *men of conscience*: we do not seek to return again to that which we regard as outlived and decayed, or to anything whatsoever that is 'unworthy of belief,' whether it goes by the name of God, virtue, truth, justice, or brotherly love; we do not allow ourselves any bridges of falsehood to old ideals; we are radically hostile to everything in us which would like to mediate and blend; we are hostile to every kind of faith, and every form of Christianity of the present day; hostile to the half-and-halfness of all romanticism and patriotism; hostile also to artist-pleasureableness, artist-consciencelessness, which would fain persuade us to worship where we no longer believe —for we also are artists; we are hostile, in short, to the whole European *femininism* (or idealism, if the word is preferred), which eternally 'draws us aloft,' and precisely thereby 'lowers us' eternally: but as men possessing *this* conscience, we still feel ourselves related to the German uprightness and piety of centuries, although we are its latest and most questionable offspring, we immoralists and godless ones of to-day; yea, we are even in a certain sense its heirs, the executors of its most fundamental wishes.

'The Rosy Dawn,' Preface, § 4.

Those who, like my readers, begin here to think seriously, to think out the subject, will have difficulty in speedily arriving at a conclusion—a sufficient reason for me to come to a conclusion, provided it has long since become sufficiently obvious what I *intend*, precisely what I intend, in making use of the dangerous watchword inscribed on the outside of my last book: '*Beyond Good and Evil.*' At any rate, it does *not* mean 'Beyond Good and Bad.'

'Genealogy of Morals,' i. 17.

OUR OUTLOOK.

The greatest modern event—that God is dead, that the belief in the Christian God has become unworthy of belief—has now begun to cast its first shadows over Europe. To the few, at least, whose eye, whose suspecting glance is strong enough and subtle enough for the spectacle, a sun seems to have set to them, some old profound truth seems to have changed into doubt; our ancient world must every day seem to them 'older,' stranger, more unreliable, more vespertine. In the main, however, one may say that the event itself is far too great, too much beyond the power of apprehension of many people, for even the report of it to have reached them, to say nothing of their capacity for knowing what is really involved and what must all collapse, now that this belief has been undermined—by being built thereon, by being buttressed thereby, by being engrafted therein; for example, our entire European morality. The prolonged excess and continuation of demolition, ruin, and overthrow which is now impending—who has yet understood it sufficiently to be obliged to stand up as the teacher and herald of such tremendously frightful logic, as the prophet of such an overshadowing, of such a solar eclipse as has probably never happened on earth before? Even we, the born riddle-readers, who as it were wait on the mountains, posted betwixt to-day and to-morrow, and engirt by the contradiction between to-day and to-morrow, we, the firstlings and premature births of the coming century, to whom especially the shadows which must forthwith envelop Europe *should* already have come in sight—how is it that even we, without genuine sympathy for this overshadowing, contemplate its advent without personal solicitude or fear? Are we still perhaps too much under the *immediate effects* of the event—and are these effects, especially as regards *ourselves,* perhaps the reverse of what was to be expected—not at all sad and depressing, but rather like a new and difficultly describable variety of light, happiness, alleviation, enlivenment, encouragement, and rosy dawn? In fact, we philosophers and 'free spirits' feel ourselves irradiated as by a new rosy dawn by the report that 'the old God is dead'; our hearts thereby overflow with gratitude, astonishment, presentiment, and expectation. At last the horizon seems once more unobstructed, granting even that it is not bright; our ships can at last start on their voyages once more, in face of every danger; every risk is again permitted to the knowing ones; the sea, our sea, again lies open before us; perhaps there was never such an open sea.

'The Gay Science,' § 343.

OUR PRECAUTIONS.

When Buddha was dead, his shadow still continued to be seen for centuries afterwards in a cave—an immense, frightful shadow. God is dead, but as the human race is constituted, there will perhaps be caves for millenniums in which his shadow will be seen. And we—we have still to get the better of his shadow!

Let us be on our guard against thinking that the world is a living being. Where could it extend itself? On what could it nourish itself? How could it grow and augment? We know approximately what the organic is: and we were meant, were we, to reinterpret the inexpressibly derivative, tardy, rare and casual which we perceive only on the crust of the earth, as the essential, universal and eternal, like those who call the universe an organism? That disgusts me.—Let us be on our guard against believing that the universe is a machine; it is assuredly not constructed for one end; we invest it with far too high an honour with the word 'machine.'—Let us be on our guard against supposing that anything so methodical as the cyclic motions of our neighbouring stars obtains generally and everywhere throughout the universe; indeed, a glance at the Milky-way induces a doubt as to whether there are not many cruder and more conflicting motions, stars with eternal rectilineal gravitating orbits, and the like. The astral arrangement in which we live is an exception, and the relatively long duration which is determined by it, has again made possible the exception of exceptions, the formation of the organic. The collective character of the world, however, is to all eternity chaos—not in the sense of the absence of necessity, but of the absence of arrangement, organisation, method, beauty, wisdom, and whatever else our æsthetic humanities are called. Judged by our reason, the unlucky casts are far oftenest the rule, nor are the exceptions the result of a hidden purpose; and the whole music-box repeats eternally its air, which can never be called a melody—and moreover the very expression 'unlucky cast' is in itself an anthropomorphising which involves blame; but how could we blame or praise the universe?—Let us be on our guard against ascribing to it heartlessness and irrationality, or their opposites; it is neither perfect, nor beautiful, nor noble, nor does it seek to be anything of the kind; it does not at all attempt to imitate man. It is altogether unaffected by any of our æsthetic or moral judgments! It is also destitute of self-preservative instinct, and in general of all instinct; it likewise knows no law.—Let us be on our guard against saying that there are laws in nature. There are only necessities; there is no one who commands, no one who obeys, no one who transgresses. When you know that there is no final goal, you know also that there is no chance, for it is only in a world with final goals that the word 'chance' has a meaning.—Let us be on our guard against saying that death is the contrary of life. The living being is only a species of the dead being, and a very rare species.—Let us be on our guard against thinking that the world produces eternally that which is new. There are no eternally enduring substances; matter is just an error similar to the God of the Eleatics.—But when shall we be at an end with our cautions and precautions? When will all these shadows of God cease to obscure us? When shall we have nature completely undeified? When shall we be permitted to commence *naturalising* ourselves with pure, newly discovered, newly redeemed nature?

'The Gay Science,' §§ 108, 109.

II. PHILOSOPHERS—TRUE AND FALSE.

FUNCTION AND QUALIFICATIONS OF THE TRUE PHILOSOPHER.

The philosopher has to be the bad conscience of his age.

What does a philosopher firstly and lastly require of himself? To overcome the spirit of his own age embodied in him, to become 'timeless.'

For such a task I required a self-discipline:—I had to adopt a hostile attitude in respect to whatever was morbid in me, including Wagner, Schopenhauer, and all modern 'humanity' under the term; moreover, a profound estrangement, coolness, and soberness with reference to everything temporary and opportune; and as my supreme desire, the eye of *Zarathustra,* an eye which, raised aloft to an immense height, surveys the whole phenomenon of man—looks *down* thereon.

'The Case of Wagner'—Preface.

It is always more obvious to me that the philosopher, as a man *indispensable* for the morrow and the day after the morrow, has ever found himself, and *has been obliged* to find himself, in contradiction to the day in which he lives; his enemy has always been the ideal of his day. Hitherto all these extraordinary furtherers of humanity whom one calls philosophers—who rarely regarded themselves as lovers of wisdom, but rather as disagreeable fools and dangerous interrogators—have found their mission, their hard, involuntary, imperative mission (in the end, however, the greatness of their mission) in being the bad conscience of their age. In putting the vivisector's knife to the breast of the very *virtues of their age,* they have betrayed their own secret: it has been for the sake of a *new* greatness of man, a new untrodden path to his aggrandisement. They have always disclosed how much hypocrisy, indolence, self-indulgence, self-neglect, and falsehood was concealed under the most venerated types of contemporary morality, how much virtue was *outlived*; they have always said, 'We must go out there, where at present *ye* are quite unfamiliar.'

'Beyond Good and Evil,' § 212.

People have always to be born to a high station, or more definitely, they have to be *bred* for it; a person has only a right to philosophy—taking the word in its higher significance—in virtue of his descent; the 'blood,' the ancestors, decide here also. Many generations must have prepared the way for the rise of the philosopher; each of his virtues must have been separately acquired, nurtured, transmitted, and embodied; not only the bold, light, delicate course and current of his thoughts, but above all, the readiness for great responsibilities, the majesty of ruling glances and proud looks, the feeling of separation from the multitude with their duties and virtues, the good-natured protection and defence of whatever is misunderstood and calumniated, whether it be God or devil, the delight in exercising supreme justice, the art of commanding, the amplitude of will, the lingering eye which rarely admires, rarely looks up, rarely loves. . . .

'Beyond Good and Evil,' § 213.

UNRELIABLENESS AND CRAFTINESS OF POPULAR PHILOSOPHERS.

That which prompts one to regard philosophers with a half-distrustful, half-mocking glance is not that one again and again discovers how innocent they are—how often and how readily they make mistakes and lose themselves, in short, their puerility and childishness—but because they do not behave with sufficient honesty, while they raise a loud and virtuous outcry immediately that the problem of conscientiousness is in the least touched upon. . . . For the most part they are even crafty advocates of prejudices which they christen 'truths.'

'Beyond Good and Evil,' § 5.

Nothing is rarer among moralists and saints than rectitude, though perhaps they say the contrary, and even *believe* it. For when a belief is more useful, more efficacious, and more convincing than *conscious* hypocrisy, hypocrisy instinctively becomes *innocence*—the first principle for understanding great saints. Among philosophers also, another species of saints, the whole business involves the necessity of only admitting certain truths, namely, those with respect to which their business has the *public* sanction—in Kantian language, the truths of the *practical* reason. They know what they are *obliged* to prove, they are practical on that point—they recognise one another by being in agreement concerning 'truths.'—'Thou shalt not lie'—in plain language, *be on your guard*, Mr. Philosopher, lest you speak the truth. . . .

'Twilight of the Idols'—'Roving Expeditions,' § 42.

III. ETHICS.

THE PROBLEM OF MORALS.

Defects in a person revenge themselves everywhere; an enfeebled, lank, obliterated, self-disavowing and disowning personality is no longer suited for anything good—it is suited least of all for philosophy. 'Selflessness' has no value either in heaven or on the earth; the great problems all demand *great love,* and it is only the strong, all-round, secure spirits, relying firmly on themselves, that are qualified for them. It makes the most material difference whether a thinker stands personally related to his problems, having his fate, his need, and his highest happiness therein; or impersonally, being only able to grasp them with the tentacles of cold, prying thinking. In the latter case nothing results therefrom—so much can be promised; for the great problems, granting that they can be grasped at all, cannot be *held* by frogs and weaklings: that has ever been their taste—a taste, besides, which they share with all high-spirited girls. How is it that I have not yet met with any one, not even in books, who seems to have stood to morality in this position, as one who knew it to be a problem, and the problem *his own* personal need, affliction, bliss, and passion? It is obvious that up to the present, morality has not been a problem at all; it has rather been the very thing with regard to which people have been in agreement after all distrust, dissension, and contradiction, the hallowed place of peace, where thinkers, laying aside even their self-conflicts, rested, recovered breath, and revived. I see no one who has ventured to criticise the estimates of moral worth. I miss, in this connection, even the attempts of scientific curiosity, and the fastidious, groping imagination of psychologists and historians, which easily anticipates a problem, and snatches at it in a hurry, without rightly knowing what it snatches at. I have with difficulty discovered some scanty odds and ends for the purpose of furnishing a *history of the origin* of these feelings and estimates of value (something different from a criticism of them, and further, something different from a history of ethical systems). I have done everything to encourage the inclination and talent for this kind of history—in vain, as it would seem to me at present. It is of little consequence with regard to the historians of morality (especially the English); they themselves are usually, quite unconsciously, under the command of a definite morality, and act unwittingly as its armour-bearers and followers; perhaps still repeating in an honest-hearted manner the popular superstition of Christian Europe, that the characteristic of moral action consists in selflessness, self-denial, self-sacrifice, or in fellow-feeling and fellow-suffering. The usual error in their preconception is that there is a consensus of opinion among human beings, or at least among civilised human beings, with regard to certain principles of morals, and they thence conclude that these propositions are unconditionally binding even upon you and me; or perhaps reversely, they come to the conclusion that no morality at all is binding, after the truth has dawned upon them that different peoples necessarily estimate moral worths differently: both of which conclusions are equally childish follies. The error of the most acute among them is that they only exhibit and criticise the probably foolish opinions of a people concerning its morality, or the opinions of mankind concerning morality universally—treating, accordingly, of its origin, its religious sanctions, the superstition of free-will, and such matters; and they actually think that by so doing they have criticised morals. But the worth of a precept, 'Thou shalt,' is still fundamentally different from, and independent of, such opinions, and must be distinguished from the weeds of error with which it has perhaps been overgrown: the worth of a medicine for a sick person is altogether independent of the question whether he has a scientific opinion with regard to it, or merely thinks of it as an old woman would do. A moral system could even have originated out of an error; with a knowledge thereof, however, the problem of its worth would not even be touched.—Consequently, no one has hitherto tested the *worth* of that most celebrated of all medicines called morality; for which purpose it is first of all necessary for us to call it in question. Well! this is just our work.

'The Gay Science,' § 345.

THE SO-CALLED SCIENCE OF MORALS.

The moral sentiment in Europe at present is perhaps as subtle, belated, divers, sensitive and refined, as the 'Science of Morals' belonging thereto is recent, initial, awkward, and coarse-fingered: an interesting contrast, which sometimes becomes incarnate and obvious in the very person of a moralist. Indeed, the expression 'Science of Morals' is, in respect to what is designated thereby, far too presumptuous and counter to *good* taste, which is generally a foretaste of more modest expressions. One ought to avow with the utmost candour *what* is still necessary here for a long time, *what* is alone proper for the present; namely, the collection of material, the comprehensive survey and classification of an immense kingdom of delicate appreciations of worth, and distinctions of worth, which live, grow, propagate, and perish—and perhaps attempts to give a clear idea of the recurring and more common forms of these living crystallisations, as preparation for a *theory of types* of morality. To be sure, people have not hitherto been so modest. All the philosophers, with a pedantic and ridiculous seriousness, demanded of themselves something very much higher, more pretentious and ceremonious, when they concerned themselves with morality as a science: they wanted to *give a basis* to morality—and every philosopher hitherto has believed that he has given it a basis; morality itself, however, has been regarded as something 'given.' How far from their awkward pride was the seemingly insignificant problem—left in dust and decay—of a description of forms of morality, notwithstanding that the finest hands and senses could hardly be fine enough for it! It was precisely owing to moral philosophers knowing the moral facts imperfectly, in an arbitrary epitome, or an accidental abridgment—perhaps as the morality of their environment, their position, their church, their *Zeitgeist*, their climate and zone—it was precisely because they were badly instructed with regard to nations, eras, and past ages, and were by no means eager to know about these matters, that they did not even come in sight of the real problems of morals—which only disclose themselves by a comparison of *many* kinds of morality. In every 'Science of Morals' hitherto, strange as it may sound, the problem of morality itself has been omitted; there has been no suspicion that there was anything problematic there! That which philosophers called 'giving a basis to morality,' and endeavoured to realise, has, when seen in a right light, been merely a learned form of good *faith* in prevailing morality, a new means of its *expression*, consequently just a matter of fact within the sphere of a definite morality, yea, in its ultimate motive, a sort of denial that it is *lawful* for this morality to be called in question—and in any case, the very reverse of the testing, analysing, doubting, and vivisecting of this faith. Hear, for example, with what innocence—almost worthy of honour—Schopenhauer represents his own task, and draw your conclusions concerning the logicalness of a 'Science' whose latest master still talks in the strain of children and old wives: 'The principle,' he says (p. 136 of the *Fundamental Problems of Morals*), 'the axiom about the purport of which all moralists are *practically* agreed: *neminem laede, immo omnes quantum potes, juva*—is *really* the proposition which all moral teachers strive to establish, . . . the *real* basis of ethics which has been sought, like the Philosopher's Stone, for centuries.' How absurdly false and sentimental this proposition is, in a world the essence of which is the Will to Power!

'Beyond Good and Evil,' § 186.

SEDUCTIVENESS OF PREVAILING MORALITY.

Morality not only has command of all kinds of frightful means for preventing critical hands and torture-instruments being applied to her; her security depends still more on a certain kind of enchantment in which she is well skilled—she knows how to 'enrapture.' She succeeds often with a single glance in paralysing the critical will, even in enticing it over to her own side; in fact, there are cases in which morality knows how to turn the critical will against itself, so that, like the scorpion, it then puts the sting into its own body. From the remotest antiquity morality has understood every devilish device of the art of persuasion: there is no orator, not even at the present day, who does not appeal to her for assistance. (Hear, for example, how our anarchists talk: how morally they talk, in order to persuade! In the end they even call themselves 'the good and just'!) From the beginning, ever since there has been talking and persuading on earth, morality has proved herself to be the greatest mistress of seduction—and as regards men of our class, she has been the veritable *Circe of philosophers*. What is the cause of it, that from Plato downwards, all philosophical architects in Europe have built in vain? Why is it that everything threatens to collapse, or already lies in ruins, which they honestly and seriously regarded as *aere perennius*?

'The Rosy Dawn,' Preface, § 3.

THE SAPPING OF FALSE MORALS.

In this book a 'subterranean being' is found at work, a boring, mining, undermining individual. One sees him—provided one has eyes for such labour in the depths—how he advances slowly, thoughtfully, and with quiet inexorableness, while the distress which the long lack of light and air always brings with it, does not betray itself too much; one could even say that he was happy at his gloomy work. Does it not seem that some faith guides him, that some consolation makes amends to him? That he perhaps wants to have his own prolonged gloom, his unintelligibility, concealedness, and enigmaticalness, because he knows that he will also have his own morn, his own salvation, his own *rosy dawn*? Certainly he will return. Do not ask him what he seeks down below; he will soon tell you himself, this Trophonios-like, underground dweller, when he has again 'become man.' One quite forgets to be silent when, like him, one has so long been a mole, and so long alone.

I undertook something which was not meant to be everybody's business: I descended into the depth, I bored into the ground, I began to investigate and sap an old *assurance* on which we philosophers have been accustomed again and again to build for a couple of millenniums, as upon the most secure foundation—notwithstanding that every structure hitherto has collapsed: I began to undermine our *assurance in morality*.

'Ibid.,' §§ 1, 2.

THE MORALITY OF SYMPATHY CALLED IN QUESTION.

I really had at heart something much more important when I wrote 'Human, All-too-Human,' than any hypothetical notion of my own or of somebody else concerning the origin of morality (or, to be more correct, I had the latter at heart only on account of an end to which it is one among many means). It was a question with me about the *worth* of morality—and on this matter I had to settle accounts almost exclusively with my great teacher Schopenhauer, to whom, as to one still living, the above-mentioned book, with its passion and secret opposition, addresses itself. It was more particularly a question about the worth of the 'unselfish' spirit, the sympathetic, self-denying, self-sacrificing instincts, which Schopenhauer especially gilded, deified, and ultramundised, to such an extent that in the end he came to regard them as 'worth in itself,' on the basis of which he *disavowed* life, and himself as well. But it was precisely against *these* instincts that an increasingly fundamental suspicion in me, an increasingly deep-sapping scepticism protested! It was precisely here that I perceived the *great* danger to humanity, its sublimest allurement and seduction—where to, do you think? to nothingness? It was precisely here that I perceived the beginning of the end, the stopping short, the retrospective weariness, the will turning itself *against* life, the last sickness announcing itself tenderly and melancholily: I regarded this continuously spreading morality of sympathy, which even attacks and prostrates philosophers, as the most portentous symptom of our already portentous European civilisation, as its indirect route to a new Buddhism? to a European Buddhism? to—*Nihilism*? This undue favouring and overvaluing of sympathy by modern philosophers is really something new: it was precisely with regard to the *worthlessness* of sympathy that philosophers hitherto were unanimous. I mention only Plato, Spinoza, La Rochefoucauld, and Kant, four minds as different from one another as possible, but agreeing on the one point: the disregard of sympathy.

The problem of the *value* of sympathy and of sympathetic morality seems at first sight to be something detached, an interrogative mark standing alone; but a person who pauses here and *learns* to question, will have the same experience as in my own case:—an immense new prospect will open up to him; a probability of a staggering nature will suggest itself; every kind of distrust, suspicion, and fear will arise; his faith in morality, in all morality, will waver; and finally a new demand will formulate itself. Let us state it here, this *new demand*: We require a *criticism* of moral valuations—*the value of these valuations has itself first to be called in question*—and for that purpose a knowledge is necessary of the conditions and circumstances out of which they have grown, under which they have developed and modified themselves (morality not only as effect, as symptom, as mask, as Tartuffism, as sickness, as misunderstanding; but also as cause, as remedy, as stimulant, as check, as poison), though such knowledge has hitherto neither existed nor been desired. The value of these 'valuations' has been taken for granted, as a matter of fact, as beyond all question; people hitherto have not had the least doubt or hesitation in rating 'a good man' as of higher worth than 'a bad man'—of higher worth for the advancement, utility, and benefit of *man* generally (including the future of man). What, if the reverse should be true? What, if there should also be a symptom of retrogression in 'the good man,' and likewise a danger, a seduction, a poison, a narcotic, by means of which the present peradventure lives *at the cost of the future*? Perhaps more comfortably, less dangerously, but also in inferior style, more meanly? . . . So that precisely morality would be to blame for it, if a *supreme degree of power and splendour* of the human type, possible in itself, should never be realised; so that morality itself would be the danger of dangers?

'Genealogy of Morals,' Preface, §§ 5, 6.

PROPER AND IMPROPER SYMPATHY.

Whether it be hedonism, pessimism, utilitarianism, eudæmonism, all those modes of thinking which measure the worth of things according to *pleasure* and *pain*—that is, according to accompanying circumstances and secondary considerations—are plausible modes of thought and naïvetés, which every one conscious of *creative* powers and an artist's conscience will look down upon with scorn, though not without sympathy. Sympathy for *you*!—to be sure, that is not sympathy as you understand it: it is not sympathy for social 'distress,' for 'society' with its sick and misfortuned, for the hereditarily vicious and defective who lie on the ground around us; still less it is sympathy for the grumbling, vexed, revolutionary slave-classes who strive after power—they call it 'freedom.' *Our* sympathy is a loftier and further-sighted sympathy:—we see how *man* dwarfs himself, how *you* dwarf him! and there are moments when we view *your* sympathy with an indescribable anguish, when we resist it, when we regard your seriousness as more dangerous than any kind of levity. You want, if possible—and there is not a more foolish 'if possible'—*to do away with suffering*; and we?—it really seems that *we* would rather have it increased and made worse than it has ever been before! Well-being, as you understand it, is certainly not a goal; it seems to us an *end*, a condition which at once renders man ludicrous and contemptible—and makes his destruction *desirable*! The discipline of suffering, of *great* suffering—know ye not that it is only *this* discipline that has produced all the elevations of humanity hitherto? The tension of soul in misfortune which communicates to it its energy, its shuddering in view of rack and ruin, its inventiveness and bravery in steadfastly enduring, interpreting, and exploiting misfortune, and whatever depth, mystery, disguise, spirit, artifice, or greatness has been bestowed upon the soul—has it not been bestowed through suffering, through the discipline of great suffering? In man *creature* and *creator* are united: in man there is not only matter, shred, excess, clay, mire, folly, chaos; but there is also the creator, the sculptor, the hardness of the hammer, the divinity of the spectator, and the seventh day—do ye understand this contrast? And that *your* sympathy for the 'creature in man' applies to that which has to be fashioned, bruised, forged, stretched, roasted, annealed, refined—to that which must necessarily *suffer*, and *is meant* to suffer? And *our* sympathy—do ye not understand what our *converse* sympathy applies to, when it resists your sympathy as the worst of all pampering and enervation?—So it is sympathy *against* sympathy!—But to repeat it once more, there are higher problems than the pleasure and pain and sympathy problems, and all systems of philosophy which deal only with these are naïvetés.

'Beyond Good and Evil,' § 225.

MAN AS AN ATTEMPT.

Spirit, as well as virtue, has strayed in its flight and made mistakes, etc., etc.

(See below, Part IV., 'Nietzsche as Prophet,' pp. 203-4.)

LIFE AS AN EXPERIMENT.

No! Life has not disappointed me! On the contrary, from year to year I find it richer, more desirable, more enigmatical—from the day on which the great emancipator came to me, the thought that life can be an experiment for the enlightened man—and not a duty, not a destiny, not a deceit!—And knowledge itself: it may be for others something different; for example, a couch of repose, or the way to a couch of repose, or an entertainment, or an idling—for me it is a world of perils and triumphs, in which the heroic sentiments also have their arena and dancing-ground. '*Life as a means to knowledge*'—with this principle in one's heart, one can not only be brave, but can even *live joyfully and laugh joyfully*! And who could understand how to laugh well and live well, who did not first of all understand war and triumph well?

'The Gay Science,' § 324.

THE WILD BEAST IN MAN.

At the bottom of all distinguished races the beast of prey is not to be mistaken, the magnificent *blond beast*, roaming wantonly in search of prey and victory. It requires from time to time the discharge of this hidden source of its nature, the animal must again show itself, it must again go back into the wilderness. Roman, Arabic, German, and Japanese nobles, Homeric heroes, Scandinavian vikings—they are all alike in this requirement. . . . The same men who are held in such strict bonds by usage, reverence, custom, gratitude, and still more by mutual watching and jealousy *inter pares* (while, at the same time, they show themselves so ingenious in deference, self-command, delicacy, fidelity, pride, and friendship in relation to one another), are not much better than wild beasts let loose towards the outside world, where what is unfamiliar, unfamiliar *people* commence. They there enjoy freedom from all social constraint; . . . like exulting monsters, they go back into the condition of innocent conscience of the beast of prey.

'Genealogy of Morals,' i. § 11.

LIFE AS EXPLOITATION.

Life itself is *essentially* appropriating, injuring and vanquishing of what is foreign and weak: it is suppression, severity, obtrusion of its own forms, incorporation, and at least, putting it most mildly, exploitation; but why should one for ever use precisely these words on which for ages a disreputable significance has been stamped? Even an organisation within which individuals deal with one another on equal terms (it is so in every healthy aristocracy) must, if it is a living and not a dying organisation, act hostilely towards other organisations in all matters wherein the several individuals restrain themselves in their dealings with one another; it must be the embodied Will to Power, it has to seek to grow, it has to endeavour to gain ground, obtain advantage, and acquire ascendency—not on account of any morality or immorality whatsoever, but because it *lives*, and because life itself *is* Will to Power.

There is nothing, however, on which the ordinary consciousness of Europeans is more unwilling to be corrected than on this matter; at present people rave everywhere, even under the guise of science, about coming conditions of society in which 'the exploiting character' will be absent: that sounds to me as if they proposed to invent a mode of life which should not exercise organic functions. 'Exploitation' does not belong to a depraved or an imperfect and primitive state of society; it belongs to the *essence* of living beings, as a fundamental organic function; it is a consequence of the intrinsic Will to Power, which is just the Will to Life.—Granting that as a theory this is an innovation, as a reality it is the original fact of history.

'Beyond Good and Evil,' § 259.

To speak of right and wrong *in itself* is destitute of significance; for *in itself* a case of injuring, violating, exploiting, or annihilating cannot naturally be a 'wrong,' inasmuch as life operates *essentially*, in its fundamental functions, in an injuring, violating, exploiting, and annihilating manner, and cannot even be conceived of without this character. One must even admit something still more momentous—namely, that from the highest biological standpoint, conditions under which rights are recognised must always be *exceptional conditions*, as partial restrictions of the intrinsic, power-seeking life-will, subordinating themselves as special expedients of the collective aim—to create *greater* units of power. A régime of rights regarded as sovereign and universal, not as an expedient in the struggle of different complexes of power with one another, but as an expedient *against* all kinds of struggle (perhaps according to the communistic pattern of Dühring, that every will should take every will as equal), would be a principle *hostile to life*, a destructive and disintegrating measure, an outrage on man's future, a sign of languishing, a bypath to nothingness.

'Genealogy of Morals,' ii. § 11.

THE WILL TO POWER.

(See below, Part IV., 'Nietzche as Prophet,' pp. 214-216.)

DUTIES AND RIGHTS IN RELATION TO POWER.

Our duties are the rights which others have upon us. How have they acquired such rights? In virtue of the fact that they regarded us as capable of making engagements and able to perform our part, because they counted us as equal and similar to themselves, and thereupon intrusted something to us, educated, instructed, and supported us. We fulfil our duty—that is to say, we justify the idea of our abilities in consideration of which all this was conferred upon us, we give back in the proportion that has been given to us. It is thus our pride which enjoins us to do our duty—we seek to restore our autonomy when we set something which we do for them over against that which others have done for us—for they have thereby encroached upon the sphere of our power, and would permanently maintain their hold thereon, unless we made a reprisal with our 'duty,' that is to say, unless we encroached on their power. The rights of others can only apply to that which is in our power; it would be unreasonable if they wanted anything from us which did not belong to us. To be more exact, however, we should say that their rights can only apply to that which they believe to be in our power, provided it is the same which we believe to be in our power. There might easily be the same error on both sides: the sentiment of duty depends on our having the same *belief* as to the extent of our power as other persons have—namely, that we *are able* to promise certain definite things, that we *can* pledge ourselves to do them. ('Freedom of Will.')

My rights are the portion of my power which others have not only permitted me to exercise, but intend that the exercise thereof shall be preserved to me. What prompts them to do so? Under certain circumstances it is their wisdom, fear, and foresight, whether it be that they expect something similar from us in return (protection of their rights), or consider a struggle with us as dangerous or unsuitable, or descry detriment to themselves in every diminution of our strength, because we would then be unsuited for an alliance with them in opposition to a hostile third power. Then, again, rights are granted by bestowal and concession. In this case others have enough, and more than enough of power, to be able to furnish therefrom and to guarantee what they furnish to him on whom they bestow it, a limited amount of the feeling of power being at the same time presupposed in him who obtains the boon. Thus rights originate—the recognised and guaranteed gradations of power. When the ratios of power shift in an essential degree, the old rights vanish and new ones form themselves; national rights demonstrate this fact by their continual lapse and regenesis. When our power diminishes to an essential extent, the sentiment of those who hitherto guaranteed our rights, changes: they consider whether they can restore to us our former measure of power; if they find themselves unable to do so, they henceforth deny our 'rights.' Similarly, when our power increases considerably, the sentiment alters of those who hitherto acknowledged it, and whose acknowledgment we no longer require; they try no doubt to depress our power to its former dimensions, they seek to encroach upon us, and summon themselves to their 'duty' in connection with the matter; but it is only useless verbosity. Where right *prevails* there is a condition and grade of power maintained, the lessening and the augmentation thereof being prevented. The right of others is the concession of our feeling of power to their feeling of power. When our power is obviously broken down and quite impaired, our rights cease; on the other hand, when our power has greatly increased, the rights of others, as we have hitherto conceded them, are no longer binding upon us.—The 'fair-dealing man' requires continually the fine tact of a pair of scales for the grades of power and rights, which, owing to the transient nature of human things, are never in equilibrium except for short intervals, but are for the most part either rising or sinking: it is consequently difficult to deal fairly, and requires much exercise, goodwill, and very much, very good *intelligence.*

'The Rosy Dawn,' § 112.

Ye say that a good cause will even sanctify war! I tell you, it is the good war that sanctifies every cause!

'Thus spake Zarathustra,' i.—'War and Warriors.'

MASTER-MORALITY AND SLAVE-MORALITY.

In strolling through the many finer and coarser forms of morality which have hitherto prevailed or yet prevail on the earth, I found certain characteristics recurring regularly in connection with one another, until at last two fundamental types betrayed themselves to me, and a fundamental distinction was brought to light. There is *Master-Morality* and *Slave-Morality.* I would at once add, however, that in all higher and compound civilisations, one finds attempts at the reconciliation of the two systems, while still oftener one finds their confusion and mutual misunderstanding; in fact, sometimes their close juxtaposition—even in the same man, in the same soul. The distinctions of moral worth have arisen either in a ruling caste, agreeably conscious of being distinct from the ruled; or among the ruled themselves, the slaves and dependants of all classes. In the first case, when it is the ruling caste that determines the conception 'good,' it is the exalted, proud disposition which is regarded as distinguishing and decisive as to the degree of rank. The noble type of man separates from himself those in whom the opposite of this exalted, proud disposition displays itself—he despises them. (Let it be noted that in this first kind of morality the antithesis 'good' and 'bad' signifies practically the same as 'noble' and 'contemptible'; the antithesis 'good' and *'evil'* has a different origin.) The despised ones are the cowards, the timid, the insignificant, those thinking merely of narrow utility, and moreover the distrustful with their constrained glances, the self-abasing, the dog-species of men who allow themselves to be misused, the mendacious flatterers, and above all, the liars—it is a fundamental belief of all aristocrats that the common people are deceitful; 'we true ones,' the nobility of ancient Greece called themselves. It is obvious that the designations of moral worth everywhere were at first applied to *men*, and were only derivatively and at a later period applied to actions. It is a bad mistake, therefore, when historical moralists start with questions such as—

'Why have sympathetic actions been praised?' The noble type of man regards *himself* as the determiner of worth, it is not necessary for him to be approved of, he passes the judgment: 'what is injurious to me is injurious in itself'; he recognises that it is he himself only that confers honour on things—he is *a creator of worth*. The type of man in question honours whatever qualities he recognises in himself: his morality is self-glorification. In the foreground there is the feeling of plenitude and power which seeks to overflow, the happiness of high tension, the consciousness of riches which would fain give and bestow; the noble man also helps the unfortunate, not (or scarcely) out of sympathy, but rather out of an impulse produced by the superabundance of power. The noble man honours the powerful one in himself, and also him who has self-command, who knows how to speak and keep silence, who joyfully exercises strictness and severity over himself, and reverences all that is strict and severe. 'Wotan has put a hard heart into my breast,' says an old Scandinavian saga: it is thus rightly expressed out of the heart of a proud viking. Such a type of man is in fact proud of *not* being made for sympathy; the hero of the saga therefore adds, by way of warning: 'He who has not had a hard heart when young, will never have a hard heart.' The noble and brave who think thus are furthest removed from the morality which sees precisely in sympathy, in acting for the good of others, or in *désintéressement*, the characteristic of morality; a belief in oneself, a pride in oneself, a fundamental hostility and irony with respect to 'selflessness,' belong as distinctly to the higher morality, as do careless indifference and precaution in presence of sympathy and the 'warm heart.'—It is the powerful who *know* how to honour; it is their art, their domain, their invention. The profound reverence for age and tradition—all law rests on this double reverence—the belief and prejudice in favour of ancestors and less favourable to new-comers, is typical of the morality of the powerful; and if, reversely, men of 'modern ideas' believe almost instinctively in 'progress' and 'the future,' and are more and more lacking in respect for the old, the ignoble origin of these 'ideas' complacently betrays itself thereby. The morality of the ruling class, however, is more especially foreign and irritating to the taste of the present day, owing to the sternness of the principle that one has only obligations to one's equals, that one may act towards beings of a lower rank, and towards all that is foreign to one according to discretion, or 'as the heart desires,' and in any case 'beyond Good and Evil.' It is here that sympathy and similar sentiments like to have a place. The capacity and obligation for prolonged gratitude and prolonged revenge—both only among equals—artfulness in retaliation, refinement of ideas in friendship, a certain necessity to have enemies (as outlets for the passions of envy, quarrelsomeness, arrogance—in fact, in order to be a good friend):—these are all typical characteristics of the noble morality, which, as we have indicated, is not the morality of 'modern ideas,' and on that account is at present difficult to realise, and also difficult to unearth and disclose.

It is different with the second type of morality, Slave-morality. Supposing that the misused, the oppressed, the suffering, the enslaved, the weary, and those uncertain of themselves should moralise, what will be the common element in their estimates of moral worth? Probably a pessimistic suspicion with regard to the whole situation of man will find expression, perhaps a condemnation of man together with his situation. The slave contemplates with disapproval the virtues of the powerful; he has a thorough scepticism and distrust, a *refinement* of distrust, of everything 'good' that is there honoured; he would like to persuade himself that the very happiness there is not genuine. On the other hand, *those* qualities are brought into prominence and into the light which tend to alleviate the existence of sufferers; it is here that the kind helping hand, the warm heart, along with sympathy, patience, diligence, submissiveness and friendliness, attain to honour; for these are the most useful qualities here, and almost the only expedients for supporting the burden of existence. Slave-morality is essentially the morality of utility. This is the seat of the origin of the celebrated antithesis 'good' and 'evil'; the notion of power and dangerousness is introduced into the evil, the ideas of dreadfulness, subtlety and strength, which do not admit of being despised. According to slave-morality, the 'evil' man also excites fear; according to master-morality, it is precisely the 'good' man who excites fear and seeks to excite it, while the 'bad' man is regarded as the contemptible being. The contrast attains its maximum when, according to the logical consequences involved, a tinge of deprecia-tion at last attaches itself to the 'good' man of slave-morality; because in any case he has to be the *safe* man: he is good-natured, easily deceived, perhaps a little stupid, *un bonhomme*. Wherever slave-morality gets the upper hand, language shows a tendency to approximate the significa-tions of the words 'good' and 'stupid.'—A last fundamental distinction: the desire for *liberty*, the instinct for happiness, and the refinements of the feeling of freedom, belong as necessarily to the domain of slave-morale and slave morality, as do enthusiasm and art in reverence and devotion to the regular symptoms of an aristocratic mode of thinking and valuing.

'Beyond Good and Evil,' § 260.

In the sphere of so-called moral valuations, there is no greater contrast than that between *master-morality* and the morality of the *Christian* conceptions of worth: the latter having grown up on a thoroughly morbid soil; while reversely, master-morality (Roman, heathen, classical, Renaissance morality) is the symbolic language of well-constitutedness, of *ascending* life, of the

Will to Power as the principle of life. Master-morality *affirms*, just as instinctively as Christian morality *denies* ('God,' 'the other world,' and 'self-renunciation' are nothing but negations). The former communicates to things out of its fulness—it glorifies, it embellishes, it *rationalises* the world; the latter impoverishes, blanches, and mars the value of things, it *denies* the world. 'The world'—a Christian term of reproach. . . . The need of *salvation*, the essence of all Christian needs, is the sincerest form of expression of *décadence*, its most convinced and painful affirmation in sublime symbols and practices. The Christian seeks to *get rid* of himself. *Le moi est toujours haïssable.*— Noble morality, master-morality, has, reversely, its roots in a triumphal *self*-affirmation —it is the self-affirming, the self-glorifying of life; it likewise requires sublime symbols and practices, but only 'because its heart is too full.' All *beautiful* art, all *great* art, belongs here; the essence of both is gratitude. On the other hand, one cannot exempt this morality from an instinctive aversion *to décadents*, a disdain, a horror even, of their symbolism: such is almost its demonstration. The noble Roman recognised Christianity as a *fœda superstitio*; I here call to mind how Goethe, the last German of noble taste, felt with regard to the cross. One seeks in vain for more valuable, more *indispensable* contrasts.

'The Case of Wagner'—Epilogue.

ASCETICISM AS A DEVICE FOR SELF-PRESERVATION.

The ascetic treats life as a wrong route which one must finally retrace to the starting-point, or as an error which one refutes, and *should* refute by action; for he requires us to go along with him, he enforces, wherever it is possible, *his* valuation of existence. What does that imply? Such an extraordinary method of valuation is not set down in human history as an exceptional case and a curiosity; it is one of the most diffused and persistent facts in existence. Read from some distant constellation, the majuscule writing of our terrestrial existence would perhaps mislead to the conclusion that the earth was the intrinsically *ascetic star*, the premises of dissatisfied, conceited, and offensive creatures, who were unable to get rid of a profound dislike of themselves, of the earth and of life generally, and who caused themselves as much pain as possible, for the pleasure of causing pain—perhaps their only pleasure. Let us but consider how regularly, how universally the ascetic priest makes his appearance in almost all periods of history; he does not belong exclusively to a particular race; he flourishes everywhere he emerges from all ranks of society. It would be a mistake to suppose that he fosters and propagates his mode of valuation by heredity; the contrary is the case —in general a profound instinct rather forbids him to propagate his species. It must be a necessity of the first importance which causes this *life-opposing* species again and again to grow up and flourish; it must surely be *an interest of life itself* which prevents such a type of self-contradiction from dying out. . . . All this is paradoxical in the highest degree. . . .

Such a self-contradiction as seems to manifest itself in the ascetic, namely, 'life *against* life,' is pure nonsense even when considered physiologically and no longer psychologically; so much is evident on the face of it. It can only be *apparent*; it must be a sort of precursory expression, an explanation, formula, arrangement, a psychological misunderstanding of something, of which for a long time the real nature could not be understood, could not be labelled *in itself* — a mere phrase crammed into an old gap of human knowledge. And to state briefly how the case stands with regard to the matter: *the ascetic ideal originates from the self-protective and self-preservative instincts of a degenerating life*, which struggles for existence, and seeks to maintain itself by all expedients; it points to partial clogging and languishing of the physiological functions, which the profoundest instincts of life that remain intact unceasingly combat with new expedients and inventions. The ascetic ideal is one of these expedients; the case is consequently precisely the reverse of what the venerators of this ideal suppose; life struggles in the ascetic ideal, and by means of it, with death, and *against* death—it is a device for the *maintenance* of life. . . . The ascetic priest is the embodied wish for a different state of existence somewhere else, and moreover, its highest embodiment, its intrinsic fervour and passion; but the very *power* of his wishing is the fetter which binds him to the present; it is precisely thereby that he becomes a tool for creating more favourable conditions for present human existence; it is precisely by this *power* that he keeps the whole herd of broken-down, bad-tempered, ill-lucked, misshapen persons, and all who suffer in themselves, firmly attached to life, by instinctively taking the lead of them, as their shepherd.

The ascetic priest must be regarded as the preordained saviour, shepherd, and advocate of the sick flock; it is only from this point of view that one can understand his extraordinary historical mission. It is his province *to rule over the sufferers*, his instinct prompts him thereto; it is there he has his special art, his superiority, his own kind of happiness. He has to be sickly himself, he has to be fundamentally related to the sick and ill-fortuned, in order to understand them, to have an understanding with them; but he has also to be strong, thoroughly master of himself, more even than of others, and unimpaired, especially in his will to power, in order to inspire confidence and dread in the sick, in order that he may be to them a stay, a resistance, a support, a constraint, a taskmaster, a tyrant, and a God. He has to defend them, the flock of which he is the shepherd—against whom? Undoubtedly, against the sound and hale, and also against their envy of the sound and hale: he must be the natural adversary and *despiser* of all barbarous, impetuous, unbridled, fierce, violent, beast-of-prey healthiness and powerfulness. The priest is the first form of the *more delicate* animal which is readier to despise than to hate. Of course he is not saved the trouble of waging war with the beasts of prey, a war of craft (of intelligence) rather than of power, as is self-evident; for that purpose it is almost necessary for him, under certain circumstances, to fashion himself into a new type of the beast of prey, or at least, *denote* such a type — a new zoological terror, in which the polar bear, the nimble, cool, expectant tiger-cat, and (not least) the fox, seem to be blended into a unity as attractive as it is awe-inspiring. Supposing necessity compels him, he assumes, perhaps, a bearishly-serious, venerable, sagacious, cool, deceitfully superior mien, and appears in the midst of the other beasts of prey themselves, as the herald and mouthpiece of mysterious powers, with the determination to sow upon this soil, wherever he can, the seeds of suffering, dissension and self-contradiction, and only too certain of his art of always getting the upper hand of *sufferers*. Undoubtedly he brings salves and balsams with him; but he has first to inflict the wound, in order to act as physician; then, in soothing the pain caused by the wound, *he at the same time poisons it*; for he is, above all, a master in such arts, this sorcerer and tamer of the beasts of prey, in whose environment everthing sound and hale necessarily becomes sick, and everything sick tame. He does, in fact, defend his sickly flock sufficiently well, this curious shepherd.

It will now be conjectured what (according to my idea) the quack-doctor instinct of life has at least *attempted* to accomplish through the ascetic priest, and for what purpose a temporary tyranny of such paradoxical and paralogical conceptions as 'guilt,' 'sin,' 'sinfulness,' 'corruption,' 'damnation' had to be used.

But is he really a *physician*, this ascetic priest? We now see why it is hardly admissible to call him a physician, notwithstanding his anxiety to feel himself a 'Saviour' and be honoured as such. It is only the suffering itself, the unpleasantness of the suffering, that is combated by him; *not* its cause, *not* the intrinsic morbidness—this must stand for our most fundamental objection to the priestly system of medication. But if we once put ourselves in the perspective, as the priest alone knows and possesses it, our admiration of all that he has there seen, sought, and found does not readily cease. *Alleviation* of suffering, consolation of every kind—such objects evince themselves as the very essence of his genius; how imaginatively has he conceived his task of comforter, how unhesitatingly and boldly has he chosen his expedients for it! Christianity, especially, might be called a great treasure-chamber of the most ingenious comforting expedients, so much refreshing, alleviating, narcotising material has been accumulated therein, so much of the most dangerous and daring nature has been attempted for this end, and how subtilely, refinedly, southernly-refinedly, it has been divined (by Christianity especially) what kind of stimulating emotions serve best to conquer, at least for a time, the deep depression, dull lassitude, and gloomy sorrowfulness of the physiologically impaired.

'Genealogy of Morals,' iii. §§ 11, 13, 15, 16, 17.

SLAVE-MORALITY AS A DEVICE FOR SELF-PRESERVATION.

If the suppressed, the down-trodden, and the violently treated, prompted by the revengeful craft of impotence, should say to themselves: 'Let us be other than the bad, let us be good! and all are good who do not act violently, who do not hurt any one, who do not attack, who do not retaliate, who leave vengeance to God, who, like us, keep themselves concealed, who always go out of the way of evil, and at the most demand very little of life, like us, the patient, the submissive, the just,'—it will really mean, when heard coolly and unprejudicedly, nothing more than this: 'We weak people are indeed weak; it is well for us not to do anything for which we are not strong enough.' This mortifying fact, however, this lowest grade of sagacity shared even by insects (which, sure enough, when in great danger simulate death in order not to do 'too much'), has invested itself, through the forgery and self-deception of impotence, with the pomp of the abdicating, inoffensive, expectant virtues, as if the weakness of the weak itself—their *character*, their action, their entire, unique, unavoidable actuality—were a voluntary rendering, something willed and chosen, a *deed*, a *merit*. This type of man *requires* the belief in a neutral, free-willed 'subject,' owing to the instinct of self-preservation and self-affirmation, through which falsehoods are accustomed to sanctify themselves. The subject (or, in more popular language, the *soul*) has perhaps so far been the best religious tenet on earth, because it has enabled the majority of mortals, the weak and suppressed of all kinds, to practise the sublime self-deception of interpreting weakness itself as freedom, the fact of their being so and so as *merit*.

Will any one look down below a little into the secret process by which *ideals are fabricated* on earth? Who has the courage to do so? Well! Here the view is open into the gloomy workshop. Wait just a moment, Sir Paul Pry and Dare-Devil; your eyes must first become accustomed to this false, changing-colour light. . . . Indeed! That will do! Speak now! What is going on below? Say it aloud, what you see, you who have such dangerous curiosity; it is *I* now who am the listener.

'I see nothing, I hear all the more. There is a cautious, insidious, suppressed whispering of people in every nook and corner. They seem to communicate lies to one another: a sugary benignity cleaves to every tone. Weakness is to be falsified into *merit*, there is no doubt; in that respect it is as you said.'

Go on!

'And the impotence which does not retaliate is to be falsified into "goodness," timorous abjectness into "humility," subjection to those whom one hates into "obedience" (to one who, they say, commands this subjection—they call him God). The inoffensiveness of the weak, their cowardice itself, of which they have ample store, their standing-at-the-door, the unavoidable necessity of their waiting—all these get good names here, such as "patience," it is even called *the* virtue; inability-to-revenge is called unwillingness-to-revenge, perhaps even forgiveness ("for *they* know not what they do—we only know what *they* do"). They also talk of "love for their enemies"—and perspire in doing so.'

Proceed!

'They are undoubtedly wretched, all these mutterers and underground forgers, though squatting warmly beside one another; but they say the wretchedness is God's choosing and the distinction he confers; the dogs which are liked best are beaten; perhaps, also, their wretchedness may be a preparation, a test, a schooling, perhaps even more—something which will one day be adjusted and paid for with immense interest in gold, no! in happiness. They call that "bliss."'

Go on!

'They now give me to understand that they are not only better than the powerful, the lords of the earth, whose spittle they must lick (*not* through fear, not at all through fear! but because God commands to honour all in authority), that they are not only better, but "have things better" also, or in any case will have things better some day. But enough! enough! I cannot stand it any longer. Bad air! bad air! This workshop in which *ideals are manufactured*—it seems to stink of so much lying.'

No! Wait a moment! You have not yet said anything of the masterpiece of these necromancers, who make whiteness, milk, and innocence out of everything black; have you not noticed what is the perfection of their *raffinement,* their boldest, subtilest, most ingenious, most mendacious, artistic stroke? Pay attention! These cellar animals, full of revenge and hatred—what do they make out of revenge and hatred? Did you ever hear these words? Trusting merely to what they say, would you suspect that you were among so many men of *ressentiment*?

'I understand. I open my ears again (ah! ah! ah! and *shut* my nose). It is now only that I hear what they have been saying so often: "We good people—*we are the just.*" What they demand—they do not call it retribution, but the "triumph of *justice*"; what they hate—is not their enemy, no! they hate "injustice," ungodliness; what they believe in and hope for is not the hope of revenge, the drunkenness of sweet revenge (Homer has called it "sweeter than honey"), but the triumph of God, the *just* God, over the godless; that which remains for them to love on earth is not their brethren in hatred, but their "brethren in love," as they say, all the good and just on the earth.'

And what do they call that which is a consolation to them in all the suffering of life—their phantasmagoria of anticipated, future bliss?

'What? Do I hear rightly? They call it "the last judgment," the coming of *their* kingdom, "the kingdom of God"; *in the meantime*, however, they live "in faith," "in love," and "in hope."'

Enough! Enough!

In faith in what? In love for what? In hope of what? These weak ones—some day or other, of course, *they* also mean to be strong, there is no doubt that some day *their* 'kingdom' is also to come—it is merely called by them 'the kingdom of God,' as has been said; they are so humble in everything! To participate *therein* it is necessary to live long, beyond death—in fact, eternal life is necessary in order that they may be indemnified eternally in 'the kingdom of God' for their life on earth, 'in faith, love, and hope.' Indemnified for what? Indemnified through what? Dante, it seems to me, made a gross mistake when, with awe-inspiring ingenuity, he placed the inscription over the gateway to his hell: 'Me too eternal love created'; in any case, over the gateway to the Christian paradise and its 'eternal bliss' the inscription: 'Me too eternal *hatred* created,' would be entitled to stand with much better right, provided that a truth would be entitled to stand over the gateway to a lie! For what is the bliss of that paradise? We might perhaps have conjectured it, but it is better that an authority not to be undervalued in such matters — Thomas Aquinas, the great teacher and saint — should expressly attest it to us. '*Beati in regno cœlesti,*' he says, gentle as a lamb, '*videbunt pœnas damnatorum, ut beatitudo illis magis complaceat.*' Or do we want to hear it in a stronger tone, out of the mouth of a triumphing church-father (Tertullian, *De Spectaculis*, c. 29)?

'Genealogy of Morals,' i. §§ 13, 14, 15.

KINSHIP OF CHRISTIANS AND UNWORTHY REVOLUTIONISTS.

Whom do I hate most among the rabble of the present day? The Socialist rabble, the Chandala apostles, who undermine the working-man's instinct, his delight, his feeling of contentedness with his petty existence—who make him envious and teach him revenge. Wrong never lies in unequal rights, it lies in the pretension to *equal* rights. What is *bad*? But I have already mentioned it: all that originates from weakness, envy, and *revenge*.—The Christian and the anarchist are of the same origin.

One may make a perfect equation between the respective characteristics of the *Christian* and the *anarchist*: their object, their instinct, is solely destructive. . . . They are both *décadents*; they are both incapable of operating otherwise than by disintegrating, poisoning, stunting, and *blood-sucking*; they both embody the instinct of *mortal hatred* of all that is, that is great, that has durability, that promises a future to life. Christianity was the vampire of the *Imperium Romanum*—in the night it undid the immense achievement of the Romans of obtaining the site for a grand civilisation.

'The Antichrist,' §§ 57, 58.

THE SLAVE INSURRECTION IN MORALS.

The Jews—'a people born for slavery,' as Tacitus and the whole ancient world say of them; 'the chosen people among the nations,' as they themselves say and believe—the Jews performed the miracle of the inversion of valuations, by means of which life on the earth received a new and dangerous charm for a couple of millenniums. Their prophets fused the terms 'rich,' 'godless,' 'evil,' 'violent,' and 'sensuous' into one idea, and for the first time coined the expression 'world' as a term of reproach. In this inversion of valuations (in which is also included the use of the term 'poor' as synonymous with 'saint' and 'friend') which the Jewish people have brought about, their significance as a people is to be found; it is with them that the *slave insurrection in morals* commences.

'Beyond Good and Evil,' § 195.

THE CONFLICT OF MASTER-MORALITY AND SLAVE-MORALITY.

The two *antithetical* valuations, 'good and bad,' 'good and evil,' have waged a fearful warfare for thousands of years. . . . The symbol of this conflict, written in letters which stand forth legible above all human history, is 'Rome against Judea, Judea against Rome': there has hitherto been no greater event than *this* conflict, *this* propounding of questions, *this* mortally hostile contradiction. The Romans perceived in the Jew something like incarnated opposition to nature, a monstrosity, as it were, the very antipodes of themselves; in Rome the Jew was regarded as '*convicted* of hatred of the entire human race'; justly so, inasmuch as it was right to connect the welfare and future of the human race with the unconditional supremacy of aristocratic valuations, Roman valuations. On the other hand, the feeling of the Jews towards Rome? One divines it by a thousand indications, but it is sufficient to call to mind the Apocalypse of St. John, the wildest of all written outbursts which the revengeful conscience has manifested. . . . The Romans were indeed the strong and noble, stronger and nobler than they have never existed, nor even been dreamt of; all their remains, all their inscriptions, enchant one, provided one divines *what* it is that there leaves its traces. The Jews, reversely, were the priestly people of *ressentiment par excellence*, in whom a politico-moral ingenuity, quite unparalleled, had enshrined itself. . . . There is no doubt at all which of them has *conquered* for the time being: one has but to consider before whom (as before the sum of all highest values) people now bow the knee in Rome itself—and not only in Rome, but almost over half the earth, wherever man has become tame, or wants to be so—before *three Jews*, as we know, and *one Jewess* (before Jesus of Nazareth, the fisherman Peter, Paul the carpet-weaver,[1] and Mary, the mother of the above-named Jesus). This is very significant: Rome has undoubtedly succumbed. To be sure, in the Renaissance there was a splendidly portentous revival of the classical ideal, of the noble mode of valuing things. Rome itself stirred like a seemingly reawakened corpse under the weight of the new Judaised Rome built over it, presenting the aspect of an œcumenical synagogue, called 'Church.' But Judea soon triumphed once more, owing to the thoroughly plebeian *ressentiment* movement (German and English) called the Reformation, together with the result which could not but follow therefrom—the re-establishment of the Church, the re-establishment also of the

[1] According to Luther's Bible, which Nietzsche follows, Paul was a 'carpet-weaver'; the English Bible makes him a tentmaker.

previous death-stillness of classical Rome. In an even more definite and profound sense than at the Reformation, Judea triumphed once more over the classical ideal when the French Revolution took place; the last political nobleness in Europe, that of *France* in the seventeenth and eighteenth centuries, then collapsed under the popular *ressentiment* instinct: never was there greater jubilation or more tumultuous enthusiasm heard, than when this took place. True enough, there happened in the midst of it the most extraordinary and unexpected event: the ancient ideal itself appeared *bodily*, and with unexampled brilliancy, before the eyes and consciences of mankind—and once more, stronger, simpler, and more forcibly than ever, there sounded forth the frightful and rapturous watchword, *the superior right of the few*, in opposition to the old lying watchword of *ressentiment, the superior right of the many*, in opposition to the will to abasement, to humiliation, to equalising, to the descent and decline of man. Napoleon, as a last indicator pointing out the *other* road, made his appearance, the most unique and belated man that has existed; and in him there appeared the incarnated problem of *the noble ideal in itself*—let us consider well *what kind* of problem it is: Napoleon, the synthesis of *brute* and *overman*.

Was that the end of the conflict? Was the greatest of all ideal antagonisms thereby settled *ad acta* for all time? Or only postponed—postponed for a long time? Must there not necessarily, some day or other, be a much more frightful and much longer prepared outbreak of the old conflagration?

'Genealogy of Morals,' i. §§ 16, 17.

NEW PHILOSOPHERS—THE HOPE OF THE FUTURE.

We who hold a belief which is different [from that of the democrats, socialists, and anarchists] —we who regard the democratic movement not only as a degenerating form of political organisation, but as equivalent to a degenerating, waning type of man, as involving his mediocrising and depreciation—where have *we* to fix our hopes? *In new philosophers*: there is no other alternative; in minds strong and original enough to introduce opposed estimates of value, to transvalue and subvert 'eternal valuations'; in forerunners, in men of the future, who in the present shall fix the constraints and fasten the knots which will compel the will of millenniums to take *new* paths. To teach man the future of humanity as *volition*, as depending on human will, and to make preparation for vast hazardous enterprises and collective attempts in rearing and educating; in order thereby to put an end to the frightful rule of folly and chance which has hitherto gone by the name of 'history' (the folly of the 'greatest number' is only its last form): for that purpose a new type of philosophers and commanders will be needed some time or other, at the very idea of which everything that has existed in the way of occult, terrible, and benevolent beings might look pale and dwarfed. The image of such leaders hovers before *our* eyes: is it lawful for me to say it aloud, ye free spirits? The conditions which one would partly have to create and partly utilise for their genesis; the presumptive methods and tests by virtue of which a soul would grow up to such an elevation and power as to feel a *constraint* to these problems; a transvaluation of values, under the new pressure and hammer of which a conscience would be steeled and a heart transformed into brass, so as to bear the weight of such responsibility; and, on the other hand, the necessity for such leaders, the dreadful danger that they might be lacking, or miscarry and degenerate—these are *our* real anxieties and glooms, ye know it well, ye free spirits! These are the heavy, distant thoughts and storms which sweep across the heaven of *our* life.

'Beyond Good and Evil,' § 203.

NOW THE FUTURE OPENS.

Ye higher men, learn this from me: in the market-place nobody believes in higher men. But if ye would preach there—well, success to you! The populace, however, says with knowing glance: 'We are all equal!'

'Ye higher men!'—so says the populace with knowing glance—'there are no higher men, we are all equal; man is man, before God—we are all equal!'

Before God! But God has died! Before the populace, however, we do not intend to be equal. Ye higher men, avoid the market-place.

Before God! But God has died! Ye higher men, God was your greatest danger.

It is only since He was laid in the grave that ye have risen from the dead. It is now only that the great noonday arrives, it is now only that the higher man becomes—master!

Take heart, ye higher men! Now for the first time the mountain of man's future is in travail. God is dead; we now want—the overman to live.

'Thus Spake Zarathustra,' iv.—'Higher Men,' §§ 1-2.

THE NATURAL SYSTEM OF RANKS AND CASTES.

Such a law-book as that of Manu sums up the experience, sagacity, and experimental morals of long centuries, it comes to a final decision, it does not devise expedients any longer. . . . At a certain point in the development of a nation, the book with the most penetrative insight pronounces that the experience according to which people are to live—*i.e.* according to which they *can* live—has at last been decided upon. The aim thereof is to garner the largest and richest harvest possible from the times of experiment and *unfortunate* experience. Consequently that which has to be specially obviated is the further persistence in experimenting, the continuation of the fluid condition of values, the testing, selecting, and criticising of values *in infinitum*. A double wall is put up against this state of things: on the one hand, *revelation*; on the other hand, *tradition*. The authority of the law establishes itself with the theses: God *gave* it; ancestors *obeyed* it. The rationale of such procedure is to oust consciousness step by step from the sphere of life recognised as correct (as *proved* by an immense and carefully sifted experience), so as to attain complete automatism of instinct—the prerequisite for every kind of superiority, for every kind of perfection in the art of living. To draw up a law-book like that of Manu means to permit a nation henceforth to get the upper hand, to become perfect, to be ambitious of the highest art of living.

The arrangement of castes, the highest, the cardinal law, is only the sanction of a *natural arrangement*, of natural legality of the highest rank, over which no arbitrariness, no 'modern idea' holds sway. In every healthy society, three mutually conditioning types, differently gravitating physiologically, separate themselves, each type having its own hygiene, its own domain of labour, its own special sentiment of perfection, its own special superiority. Nature, and *not* Manu, separates those mainly intellectual, those mainly endowed with muscular and temperamental strength, and those neither distinguished for the one nor the other, the mediocre third class, from one another; the latter being the great number, the former the select individuals.

The highest caste—I call them *the fewest*—

have, as being the perfect caste, the privileges of the fewest: in this connection it belongs to them to represent happiness, beauty, and goodness on the earth. It is only the most intelligent men who have licence to beauty, to the beautiful; it is only in them that goodness is not weakness. *Pulchrum est paucorum hominum:* the good is a privilege. But nothing can be less permissible to them than bad manners or a pessimistic glance, an eye that *disfigures* what it sees, or indignation even at the general aspect of things. Indignation is the privilege of the Chandala; pessimism likewise. '*The world is perfect*'—thus speaks the instinct of the most intelligent men, the affirmative instinct; 'imperfection, everything *inferior* to us, distance, pathos of distance, and the Chandala himself, belong even to this perfection.' The most intelligent men, as being the *strongest*, find their happiness in that wherein others would find their ruin: in the labyrinth, in severity towards themselves and others, in effort; their delight is self-conquest; with them asceticism becomes nature, requirement, and instinct. The difficult task is regarded by them as a privilege; to play with burdens which crush others to death, as a *recreation*; knowledge—a form of asceticism.—They are the most venerable type of men; that does not, however, prevent them being also the most cheerful, the most amiable men. They rule, not because they want to do so, but because they *are* rulers; they are not at liberty to hold the second place.

The second caste—they are the attendants of justice, the guardians of order and security; they are the noble warriors, including the king especially, as the highest embodiment of warrior, judge, and vindicator of the law. The second caste are the executive of the most intelligent caste, the most closely associated with them, relieving them of all that is *coarse* in the work of ruling, their retinue, their right hand, their best disciples.—In all this there is nothing arbitrary, nothing 'artificial'; what is *otherwise* is artificial—nature is then spoiled. The arrangement of castes, the *gradation of ranks*, merely formulates the supreme law of life; the distinction of the three types is necessary for the maintenance of society, for making the higher and the highest types possible—the *inequality* of rights is really the condition of there being rights at all. A right is a privilege. In his sphere of existence every one has his privilege.

Let us not undervalue the privileges of the *mediocre*. Life always becomes harder towards the summit—the cold increases, the responsibility increases. A high civilisation is a pyramid, it can only stand on a broad basis; it has, first of all, a strongly and soundly consolidated mediocrity for a prerequisite. Handicraft, trade, agriculture, *science*, the main part of art—in a word, the whole compass of business activity—is really compatible only with an average amount of ability and aspiration; such pursuits would be out of place among exceptional men, the instinct appropriate thereto would conflict with aristocratism as much as with anarchism. There is a provision in nature for a person being a public utility, a wheel, a function; it is *not* society, it is the kind of *happiness* of which alone the largest number are capable, that makes intelligent machines out of them. To the mediocre it is a happiness to be mediocre; to them superiority in one thing, specialism, is a natural instinct. It would be altogether unworthy of a profounder mind to see in mediocrity itself an objection. It is itself the *first* necessity in order that there may be exceptional men; a high civilisation is conditioned by it.

'The Antichrist,' § 57.

THE ESSENCE OF A TRUE ARISTOCRACY.

The essential thing in a good and healthy aristocracy is *not* to regard itself as a function either of royalty or of the community, but as the *significance* and highest justification thereof; it must acquiesce, accordingly, with a good conscience in the sacrifice of a legion of individuals, who, *for the sake of it*, have to be suppressed and reduced to incomplete men, to slaves and tools. Its fundamental belief must really be that society is *not* entitled to exist for its own sake, but only as a substructure and scaffolding, by means of which a select race of beings may elevate themselves to their higher duties, and, in general, to a higher *existence*—comparable to the sun-seeking, climbing plants in Java (they are called *Sipo matador*), which encircle an oak so long and so often with their arms, until at last, high above it, but still supported by it, they can spread their tops in the open light and manifest their felicity.

'Beyond Good and Evil,' § 258.

THE OVERMAN.

I teach you the overman. Man is something that is to be surpassed, etc. etc.

(See below, Part IV., 'Nietzsche as Prophet,' pp. 192-195).

GOOD AND BAD.

What is good? All that elevates the feeling of power, the will to power, and power itself in man.

What is bad? All that proceeds from weakness.

What is happiness? The feeling that power *increases*—that resistance is being overcome.

Not contentedness, but more power; *not* peace generally, but war; *not* virtue, but capacity (virtue in the Renaissance style: *virtù*, open-air virtue).

The weak and defective are to go to the wall (the first principle of *our* charity). And we are to help them thereto.

What is more injurious than any crime? Practical sympathy for all the defective and weak—Christianity.

'The Antichrist,' § 2.

NEW COMMANDMENTS.

Do I advise you to love your neighbour—the nearest human being? I advise you rather to flee from the nearest, and love the furthest human being!

Higher than love to the neighbour is love to the furthest and future human being.

It is not the neighbour that I recommend to you, but the friend. Let the friend be the good cheer of the earth to you, and a foretaste of the overman.

Let the future and the furthest be the motive of thy to-day; in the friend thou must love the overman as thy motive.

'Thus Spake Zarathustra,' i.—'Loving One's Neighbour.'

He who is emancipated in spirit has still to purify himself. Many traces of the prison and the mould still remain on him; his eye has yet to become pure.

By my love and hope, I conjure thee: cast not away the hero in thy soul! Maintain holy thy highest hope!

Ibid.—'The Tree on the Mountain.'

Ye should love peace as a means to new war; and the short peace more than the long.

I do not exhort you to work, but to fight. I do not exhort you to peace, but to victory. Let your work be a battle, let your peace be a victory!

Ye should only have enemies to be hated, not enemies to be despised. Ye must be proud of your enemies; then the successes of your enemies are also your successes.

Ibid.—'War and Warriors.'

The man of enlightenment must be able not only to love his enemies, but to hate his friends.

Ibid.—'The Bestowing Virtue.'

When ye have an enemy, do not return him good for evil, for that would make him ashamed; but prove that he has done something good to you.

And when a great injustice has been done you, do at once five more small ones! He on whom injustice presses alone is hideous to behold.

Were ye ever aware of this? Shared injustice is half justice. And he who can bear it must take the injustice on himself.

Ibid.—'The Bite of the Adder.'

Man must be trained for war, and woman for the relaxation of the warrior; all else is folly.

Ibid.—'Old and Young Girls.'

Thou shouldst build living monuments to thy victory and emancipation.

Thou shouldst not only propagate thyself onward, but upward! May the garden of marriage help thee thereto!

Ibid.—'Child and Marriage.'

Die at the right time: so teaches Zarathustra.

He who has a goal and an heir, wants death at the right time for the goal and the heir.

And out of reverence for the goal and the heir, he will hang up no more withered wreaths in the sanctuary of life.

That your dying, my friends, may not be a reproach to man and to the earth—that is what I solicit from the honey of my soul.

In your dying, your spirit and your virtue should continue to shine like an evening after-glow around the earth; otherwise your dying has not been a success.

Ibid.—'Voluntary Death.'

This new table, my brethren, I put up for you: '*Become hard!*'

Ibid. iii.—'The Old and New Tables,' § 29.

(See also below, Part. IV., 'Nietzsche as Prophet,' pp. 234-244.)

IV. ÆSTHETICS.

THE METAPHYSICS OF ART.

This one thing at least must be clear to us, to our humiliation and exaltation, that the entire comedy of art is not by any means performed for our betterment and culture, and that we are just as little the true authors of this art-world; we may rather assume with regard to ourselves that its true author uses us as pictures and art projections, and that we have our highest dignity in our significance as works of art—for only as an *aesthetic phenomenon* is existence and the world eternally *justified*; while of course our consciousness of this our specific significance hardly differs from the kind of consciousness which the soldiers painted on canvas have of the battle represented thereon. Hence, all our knowledge of art is in reality illusory, because, as knowing persons, we are not one and identical with the being who, as the sole author and spectator of this comedy of art, prepares a perpetual entertainment for himself. Only in so far as the genius, in the act of artistic production, coalesces with the primordial artist of the world does he get a glimpse of the eternal essence of art; for in this state he is in a marvellous manner like the weird picture in the fairy-tale, which can at will turn its eyes and behold itself; he is now simultaneously subject and object, poet, actor, and spectator. . . .

Here it is necessary to swing ourselves with a daring bound into a metaphysic of art. I repeat, therefore, that it is only as an æsthetic phenomenon that existence and the world appears justified; and in this sense it is precisely the function of tragic myth to convince us that even the ugly and discordant is an artistic game which the will, in the eternal fulness of its joy, plays with itself. But this difficultly comprehensible proto-phenomenon of Dionysian art becomes in a direct way singularly intelligible, and is immediately apprehended in the wonderful significance of *musical dissonance*; just as in general it is music alone, placed in contrast to the world, which can give us an idea as to what is meant by the justification of the world as an æsthetic phenomenon. The joy which the tragic myth creates has the same origin as the joyful sensation of dissonance in music. The Dionysian, with its primitive joy perceived in pain itself, is the common source of music and of tragic myth.

'Birth of Tragedy,' §§ 5 and 24.

Once on a time Zarathustra also cast his imagination beyond human beings, like back-worlds-men. The world then seemed to me the product of a suffering and tortured God.

The world seemed to me the dream and fancy of a God—coloured vapours to the eyes of a divinely dissatisfied being.

Good and evil, and pleasure and pain, and I and thou—they seemed to me coloured vapours to creative eyes. The Creator wanted to look away from himself—so he created the world.

It is intoxicating pleasure for the sufferer to look away from his suffering and lose himself. The world once seemed to me intoxicating pleasure and losing of myself.

This world, the eternally imperfect, the image, the imperfect image of an eternal contradiction—an intoxicating pleasure to its imperfect creator: thus did the world seem to me.

Thus, once on a time, did I also cast my imagination beyond human beings, like all the backworlds-men. In reality, beyond human beings?

Ah, my brethren, the God whom I created was a human product and a human mania, like all the Gods!

It was a man, and only a poor specimen of man and ego. Out of my own ashes and flame, it came to me, that spectre. Verily, it did not come to me from the beyond!

What happened, my brethren? I overcame my suffering mood, I carried my ashes to the mountain. I learned to make for myself a brighter flame. And lo! the spectre *vanished*!

'Thus Spake Zarathustra,' i. 'Backworlds-men.'

THE BEAUTIFUL.

Nothing is more conditioned than our sense of the *beautiful.* Those who would think of it as detached from the delight of man in man, immediately lose their footing. 'The beautiful in itself' is merely an expression. In the beautiful, man posits himself as the standard of perfection; in select cases he adores himself as such. A species cannot do otherwise than thus acquiesce solely in itself. Its *fundamental* instincts of self-maintenance and self-expansion still radiate in such sublimities. Man believes the world itself to be suffused with beauty; he *forgets* that he is the cause thereof. He alone has endowed it with beauty; alas! only with a very human, all-too-human beauty. In reality, man mirrors himself in things; he counts everything beautiful that reflects his likeness: the verdict 'beautiful' is man's *conceit of his species.*

'Twilight of the Idols'—'Roving Expeditions,' § 18.

THE UGLY.

Nothing is beautiful in itself, man only is beautiful: all æsthetics rest on this *naïveté*; it is their first truth. Let us at once add the second: nothing is *ugly* except the *degenerating* man. The domain of æsthetic judgments is therewith determined. Whatever is ugly weakens and troubles man. It reminds him of deterioration, danger and impotence; he actually suffers loss of power thereby. Whenever man is at all depressed, he has a sense of the proximity of something 'ugly.' His sense of power, his will to power, his feeling of pride—they all sink with the ugly and rise with the beautiful. The ugly is instinctively understood as a sign and symptom of degeneration; that which reminds one in the remotest manner of degeneracy prompts us to pronounce the verdict 'ugly.' Every indication of exhaustion, heaviness, age, or lassitude, every kind of constraint, such as cramp or paralysis; and above all, the odour, colour, and resemblance of decomposition or putrefaction, be it attenuated even to a symbol—it all calls forth the same reaction, the evaluation 'ugly.' *Hatred* is thereby excited; what is it that man hates there? But it is quite obvious: it is *the decline of his type.* The hatred is inspired by the profoundest instinct of the species; there is horror, foresight, depth, and wide prospect therein —it is the profoundest of all hatreds. On account thereof, art is *profound.*

Ibid., § 19.

'L'ART POUR L'ART.'

The hostility to the end in art is always hostility to the *moralising* tendency in art, to its subordination under morality. *L'art pour l'art* means: 'The devil take morality!'—But this hostility itself still betrays the domination of prejudice. When the ends of the ethical preacher and the improver of mankind have been excluded from art, it still does not by any means follow that art generally is without an end, without a goal, without meaning; in short, *l'art pour l'art*—a serpent which bites its own tail. 'No end at all, rather than a moral end!' is what mere passion says. A psychologist, on the other hand, asks: What does art do? Does it not praise? does it not glorify? does it not select? does it not bring into prominence? In all these cases it *strengthens* or *weakens* certain estimates of worth. Is this only a contingent matter? an accident? something with which the instinct of the artist should not be at all concerned? Or rather, is it not the prerequisite which *enables* the artist to do something? Is his fundamental instinct concerned with art, or is it not rather concerned with the significance of art, namely, *life? a desirableness of life?*—Art is the great stimulus to life; how could it be understood as purposeless, as aimless, as *l'art pour l'art*?

Ibid., § 24.

PARALLELISM OF ÆSTHETICS AND ETHICS.

An age has either the virtues of *ascending* life, and then, from its innermost nature, it resists the virtues of declining life; or it is itself an epoch of declining life, and then it requires the virtues of decline—it hates everything that justifies itself solely by plenitude and superabundance of strength. Æsthetics is indissolubly bound up with these biological presuppositions: there is *décadence* æsthetics and *classical* æsthetics—the 'beautiful in itself' is a chimera, like all idealism.

'The Case of Wagner—Epilogue.'

V. FIRST AND LAST THINGS.

IN THE BEGINNING.

The most serious parody I ever heard is this: 'In the beginning there was nonsense, and the nonsense *was* with God, and the nonsense was God.'

'Miscellaneous Opinions and Apophthegms,' § 22.

EXOTERIC AND ESOTERIC TEACHING.

Our deepest insights must—and should!—appear as follies, and under certain circumstances as crimes, when in an unauthorised manner they reach the ears of those who are not disposed and predestined for them. The exoteric and esoteric, as they were formerly distinguished by philosophers—among the Indians, as among the Greeks, Persians, and Mussulmans, in short, wherever people believed in gradation of rank and *not* in equality and equal rights—are not so much in contradistinction to one another in respect to the exoteric class standing without, and viewing, estimating, measuring, and judging from the outside and not from within; the more essential distinction is that the class in question views things from below upwards, while the esoteric class views them *from above downwards*! . . . That which serves the higher class of men for nourishment or refreshment, must be almost poison to a very different and much lower species of human beings. The virtues of the common man would perhaps denote vices and weaknesses in a philosopher; it might be possible for a highly developed man, supposing him to degenerate and go to wreck, to acquire qualities thereby (and in no other way), on account of which he would have to be honoured as a saint in the lower world into which he had sunk. There are books which have a reverse value for the soul and the health, according as the inferior soul and the low vital force, or the higher and more powerful, made use of them: in the first case they are dangerous, disturbing, unsettling books; in the other case they are herald-calls which summon the bravest to *their* bravery. Books for everybody are always bad-smelling books, the odour of the masses always cleaves to them. Where the people eat and drink, and even where they reverence, it is accustomed to stink. One should not go into churches when one wants to breathe *pure* air.

'Beyond Good and Evil,' § 30.

THE SOLAR PATH OF AN IDEA.

When an idea rises on the horizon the temperature of the soul is usually very cold. It is only gradually that the idea develops its warmth, which is greatest (that is to say, it has its greatest effects) when the belief in the idea is already on the decline.

'The Wanderer and his Shadow,' § 207.

THE POPULAR ATTITUDE TO INDEPENDENT MINDS.

When we take the decisive step and enter upon the way which is called 'one's own way,' a secret suddenly discloses itself: every one who has been friendly and familiar with us—they all prided themselves hitherto on a certain superiority over us—is shocked. The best of them are indulgent, and wait patiently in order that we may again find the 'right way'—they know it, of course! Others mock, and pretend we have become temporarily crazy, or they point spitefully to a seducer. Worse ones declare us conceited fools, and seek to disparage our motives; while the worst of all see in us their bitterest enemies, persons who thirst for revenge on account of a long dependence upon them—and they are afraid of us.—What to do under the circumstances? I would suggest that we should initiate our prerogative by assuring to all our acquaintances amnesty for sins of every kind for a year in advance.

'The Rosy Dawn,' § 484.

THE BAD CONSCIENCE OF THE GOOD.

You imagine that whatever is good has always had a good conscience?—Science, however, which is certainly a great good, has come into the world without anything of the kind, and quite destitute of pathos; it has rather introduced itself clandestinely by indirect routes, with veiled or masked head, like a criminal, and having always at least the *feeling* of an interloper. The good conscience involves as a preliminary stage the bad conscience —and not as its antithesis; for whatever is good has at one time been new: it has consequently been unwonted, contrary to custom, and *immoral*, and has gnawed at the heart of its fortunate inventor like a worm.

'Miscellaneous Opinions and Apophthegms,' § 90.

THE QUESTION OF TRUTH.

In the market-place one convinces by gestures, but reasons make the populace distrustful.

And when the truth has once triumphed there, ask yourselves with good distrust: 'What powerful error has fought for it?' . . .

Incapableness of lying is still far from being love to truth. Be on your guard! . . .

I do not believe in thoroughly cooled spirits. He who cannot lie does not know what truth is.

'Thus Spake Zarathustra,' iv.—'Higher Men,' § 9.

THE PROGRESS OF FREEDOM OF SPIRIT.

One cannot better illustrate the difference between the earlier and the present freedom of spirit than by recollecting the saying which required all the intrepidity of the past century to recognise and express it, which, however, when measured by the insight of the present day, sinks to an involuntary naïveté—I mean the saying of Voltaire: '*Croyez-moi, mon ami, l'erreur aussi a son mérite.*'

'Miscellaneous Opinions and Apophthegms,' § 4.

DANCING—A SIMILE OF HIGH CULTURE.

At present it is regarded as the distinguishing mark of high culture, when a person possesses the power and agility to be as thorough and strict in discernment, as in the capacity to give, as it were, a start of a hundred paces to poetry, religion, and metaphysics, and yet to feel their power and beauty. A position of the kind, 'twixt two such different claims, is very difficult, because science insists on the absolute supremacy of its methods, and if its insistence is not complied with, there arises the other danger of an impotent oscillation backwards and forwards from one tendency to another. However, to communicate by means of a simile an insight towards the solution of this difficulty, one may call to mind that a *dance* is not the same as languidly staggering to and fro from one tendency to another. High culture seems to be like a bold dance; consequently, as we have said, much power and agility are necessary thereto.

'Human, All-too-Human,' § 278.

THE PROPER RECIPE FOR DESTROYING ERROR.

Those who seek to free mankind from a misconception, do not usually satisfy themselves with refuting it and extracting from it the illogical worm; on the contrary, after the worm has been killed, they also throw the whole fruit among the dirt, in order to make it unsightly in people's eyes, and thereby inspire disgust for it. They thus imagine they have found the means for making the 'resurrection on the third day' impossible, which is so usual with refuted conceptions.—They are in error; for it is precisely on the *soil of ignominy*, in the midst of filth, that the kernel of misconception germinates most rapidly. One should not then deride and befoul what one intends to abolish definitely; one should *place it* respectfully *on ice*, again and again, in consideration of the fact that misconceptions have a very tough life. One must here act according to the maxim: 'One refutation is no refutation.'

'The Wanderer and his Shadow,' § 211.

INCORRIGIBLENESS OF THE IDEALIST.

The idealist is incorrigible: if one casts him out of his heaven he makes an ideal out of his hell. One may disillusion him, and lo!—he embraces the disillusionment no less ardently than he previously embraced his hope. In so far as his propensity belongs to the great incorrigible propensities of human nature, it may produce tragic events, and ultimately become the subject of tragedies, which have to do precisely with the incorrigible, inevitable, and unavoidable in human lot and character.

'Miscellaneous Opinions and Apophthegms,' § 23.

OPTIMISM AND PESSIMISM OUTGROWN.

Away with the wearisomely hackneyed terms Optimism and Pessimism! For there is daily less and less occasion to use them; it is only the babblers for whom they are still so indispensable. For why, in all the world, should anybody be an optimist, unless he has a God to defend, who *must* have created the best of worlds, if He be divine goodness and perfection? What thinking man is there, however, who still requires the hypothesis of a God?—But neither is there occasion for a pessimistic confession of faith, if it is not a person's interest to be vexed with the advocates of God (the theologians, or the theologising philosophers), and unless he wishes to assert emphatically the counter-allegation, that evil rules, that non-delight is greater than delight, that the world is a piece of bungling, the manifestation of an ill-will to life. But who concerns himself any longer about the theologians—except the theologians?—Apart from theology and its contentions, it is obvious that the world is neither good nor bad (to say nothing of best or worst), and that these conceptions 'good' and 'bad' have significance only in relation to man; indeed, perhaps even here they are not authorised in the manner in which they are ordinarily used. We must by all means rid ourselves alike of the reviling and glorifying mode of contemplating the world.

'Human, All-too-Human,' § 28.

THE SEASONS OF HUMAN LIFE.

The comparison of the four ages of life with the four seasons of the year is a venerable folly. Neither the first twenty nor the last twenty years of life correspond to a season, unless one is content with the comparison of such striking hues as the whiteness of the hair with that of snow. The first twenty years are a preparation for life generally, for the whole year of life, as a sort of long New Year's Day; while the last twenty serve to review, assimilate, adjust, and harmonise all that has been previously experienced, as is done in a less degree with reference to the whole past year on every Old Year's Day. In between, however, there is actually a period which suggests a comparison with the seasons of the year—the period from the twentieth to the fiftieth year (to count here in the gross according to decades; it is obvious that every one must refine these rough formulæ according to his own experience). These three times ten years correspond to three seasons of the year—summer, spring, and autumn; human life is without a winter, unless we call the hard, cold, lonesome, unpromising, unfruitful *periods of sickness* (which unfortunately not seldom supervene) the winter season of man. The twenties —warm, troublesome, stormy years, germinating luxuriously, involving fatigue, in which one considers the day happy in the evening, after it is over, when one wipes the sweat from the brow; years in which labour seems to us hard, but necessary—the twenties are the *summer* of life. The thirties, on the other hand, are its *spring;* years with the air alternately too hot and too cold, always agitated and stimulating, with gushing sap, foliage, and the perfume of blossoms everywhere, with many enchanting nights and mornings—the work, to which the song of the birds awakens us, being a genuine labour of love, a sort of enjoyment of our own vigour, strengthened by foretasting hopes. Finally the forties: mysterious, like everything stationary, resembling a high broad plateau over which blows a fresh breeze, with a clear cloudless heaven above, which gazes throughout the day and into the night, ever with the same serenity, the time of harvest and of the most cordial cheerfulness—it is the *autumn* of life.

'The Wanderer and his Shadow,' § 269.

THE DEFECT OF ACTIVE MEN.

Active men generally lack the higher activity —I mean individual activity. They are active as officials, merchants, scholars, that is to say, as members of a species, but not as wholly distinct, single, and individual men—in this respect they are lazy.—It is the misfortune of the active that their activity is almost always somewhat senseless. For example, one is not at liberty to inquire as to the object of the restless activity of the gold-accumulating banker; it is unreasonable. The active roll like a stone, in accordance with the stupidity of mechanics.—All men are still divided, as they have ever been, into bond and free; for whoever has not two-thirds of the day to himself is a slave, no matter what he may be otherwise: statesman, merchant, official, scholar.

'Human, All-too-Human,' i. § 283.

PLEASURABLE WORK AND ENNUI.

In seeking work for the sake of the pay, almost all men are alike at present in civilised countries; to all of them work is a means, and not itself the goal; on which account they are not very select in the choice of the work, provided it yields them a rich return. Still, there is a rarer species of men, who would go to perdition rather than work without *delight* in their labour: the fastidious people, difficult to satisfy, whose purpose is not served by a rich return, unless the work itself be the reward of all rewards. Artists and contemplative men of all kinds belong to this rare species of human beings; moreover, also the idlers who pass their life in hunting and travelling, or in love affairs and adventures. They all seek toil and trouble as far as these are associated with delight, and the hardest, severest toil, if it be necessary. In other respects, however, they are men of resolute indolence, even should impoverishment, dishonour, and danger to health and life be associated therewith. They are not so much afraid of *ennui* as of labour without pleasure; in fact they require a deal of *ennui*, if their work is to succeed with them. To the thinker and to the inventive spirit, *ennui* is the 'calm' of the soul which precedes the happy voyage and the dancing breezes; he must endure it, he must *await* the effect which it has upon him; it is precisely this influence which lesser natures cannot possibly experience! It is common to scare away *ennui* in every way, just as it is common to labour without pleasure.

'The Gay Science,' § 42.

THE PHILOSOPHER AND MARRIAGE.

It is ludicrous when a company of penniless persons decree the abolition of hereditary rights; and it is not less ludicrous when childless persons work at the practical legislation of a country; they have not, in fact, enough of substance in their ships to sail safely into the ocean of the future. But it seems just as preposterous, when he who has chosen the most general knowledge and the evaluation of collective existence for his problem, burdens himself with personal considerations for a family, for the support, security, and respect of wife and child, and thereby stretches a gloomy veil in front of his telescope, through which hardly a ray of the distant stellar world can penetrate. So I also arrive at the conclusion that, in matters of the highest philosophical import, all married men are suspicious.

'Human, All-too-Human,' § 436.

As to whether the free spirits will have wives, I believe generally that, like the soothsaying birds of antiquity, they will prefer, as the true thinkers and truth-speakers of the present, *to fly singly*.

Ibid., § 426.

WOMAN'S ATTITUDE TO THE FREE SPIRIT.

The natural inclination of women to quiet, uniform, happily attuned existence and intercourse, the oil-like and soothing nature of their influence on the sea of life, operates involuntarily adverse to the heroic inner impulse of the free spirit. Without being aware of it, women act like a person who would remove the stones from the path of a mineralogist, lest his feet should come in contact with them, while he has gone forth precisely *for the purpose* of coming in contact with them.

Ibid., § 431.

Just as mothers have only sense and eye for

the visible and sensible pains of their children, so the wives of men with lofty aspirations cannot resign themselves to seeing their husbands suffering, impoverished, and slighted; while perhaps this is not only the token of the right choice of their attitude to life, but already the pledge that their lofty aims *must* some day or other be realised. Women always intrigue in secret against the higher souls of their husbands; they seek to cheat them out of the future for the sake of a painless and comfortable present.

Ibid., § 434.

THE CALAMITY OF IMPROPER MARRIAGES.

If I were a God, and a benevolent God, men's *marriages* would make me more impatient than anything else. An individual can advance far, far in his seventy, yea, in his thirty years; it is astonishing even to Gods! But when one sees how he exposes the inheritance and legacy of this struggle and triumph, the laurel of his humanity, wherever there is a girl to pluck it in pieces, when one sees how well he understands how to acquire, and how badly he understands how to preserve, yea, how he does not even think of the fact that by procreation he could prepare a still more triumphant life—one becomes impatient, as remarked above, and says to oneself: 'There can be nothing made out of humanity in the long run; the individuals are squandered, the event of marriage makes all the rationality of a great march of mankind impossible; let us cease being the eager spectators and dupes of this aimless spectacle!'—It was in this frame of mind that the Gods of Epicurus formerly withdrew themselves into their divine tranquillity and bliss: they were tired of man and his love affairs.

'The Rosy Dawn' § 150.

THE ATTITUDE AT DEATH INDIFFERENT.

The way in which a man thinks of death in the full bloom of his life and strength is certainly very significant and evidentiary with regard to that which one calls his character; but the hour of death itself, his attitude on his dying bed, is almost indifferent in that respect. The exhaustion of the sinking existence, especially when old people die, the irregular or insufficient nourishment of the brain during this last period, the occasionally excessive violence of the pain, the inexperience and novelty of the whole situation, and even, too often, the onset and return of superstitious impressions and anxieties, as if so much depended on the dying, and as if there were bridges of the most awful kind to cross in this connection—all these matters prevent death being used as a testimony with regard to a person's life. Moreover, it is not true that a dying person is in general *more honourable* than a person in ordinary vigour; on the contrary, almost every dying person is liable to be allured by the solemn attitude of the company, and the restrained or flowing torrents of tears and emotions, to an alternating conscious and unconscious comedy of conceitedness. The seriousness with which every dying person is treated has undoubtedly been the very finest enjoyment of his life to many a poor despised devil, and a sort of indemnification and partial payment for much privation.

'Miscellaneous Opinions and Apophthegms,' § 88

IRRATIONAL DEATH.

Natural death is death destitute of rationality, it is really *irrational* death, in which the pitiable substance of the shell determines how long the kernel is to endure; in which, consequently, the pining, sick, sottish prison-warder is the authority who designates the hour when his noble prisoner is to die. Natural death is the suicide of nature, that is to say, the annihilation of the most rational part by the most irrational, which is united with it. Only under religious illumination can it appear the reverse; because then, as is only fair, the higher reason (God) gives the command, to which the lower reason has to adjust itself. Apart from religion, natural death is not worthy of any glorification. — The enlightened regulation and control of death belongs to the morality of the future—at present quite intangible and seemingly immoral, the appearance of the rosy dawn of which, however, must cause indescribable happiness.

'The Wanderer and his Shadow,' § 185.

ENCOURAGEMENT.

Forward then on wisdom's road, with firm step and good confidence! Whatever be thy state, serve as a source of experience to thyself! Cast away dissatisfaction with thy nature, pardon thyself on account of thine own *ego*, for in any case thou hast in thyself a ladder with a hundred rounds, on which thou canst ascend to knowledge. The age into the midst of which thou regretfully feelest thyself cast, counts thee happy for such good fortune; it calls out to thee that at present experiences still fall to thy lot which men of later times must perhaps dispense with. Do not despise it to have been religious; fathom it fully that thou hast had a genuine access to art. Canst thou not, precisely by these experiences, follow more intelligently immense stretches of the path of earlier humanity? Is it not precisely on the *very soil* which occasionally displeases thee so much, the soil of inaccurate thinking, that many of the most splendid fruits of ancient civilisation have grown? One must have loved religion and art as mother and nurse—otherwise one cannot become wise. But one must see beyond them, one must be able to outgrow them; if one remains under their spell one does not understand them. In like manner must history be familiar to thee, and the cautious game with the scales: 'on the one hand—on the other hand.' Wander back, treading in the footsteps by which humanity has made its great, suffering journey through the desert of the past: thou wilt thus learn most surely where it is that future humanity cannot, or should not again walk. And when thou seekest, with all thy power, to divine how the knot of the future has to be tied, thine own life acquires the value of an instrument and expedient of knowledge. It is in thy power to make all thy experiences—thy attempts, errors, mistakes, illusions, passions, thy love and thy hope—subserve to thy aim. Thy aim is to become thyself a chain of necessary culture-links, and from their necessity to infer the necessity in the process of general culture. When thy glance has become strong enough to discern the bottom of the dark well of thy being and experience, the distant constellations of future civilisations will also perhaps become visible to thee in that mirror. Dost thou think that such a life, with such an aim, is too painful, too devoid of charms? Then thou hast not yet learned that no honey is sweeter than that of knowledge, and that the lowering clouds of tribulation must yet serve thee as udders out of which thou wilt milk the milk for thy refreshment. When age comes, then only wilt thou rightly perceive how thou hast obeyed the voice of nature, that nature which rules the whole world by means of delight: the same life which has its apex in age has also its apex in wisdom, in the soft, solar radiance of a constant intellectual cheerfulness; thou meetest both, age and wisdom, on the same mountain ridge of life—thus nature has willed it. It is then the time—and no occasion for displeasure—for the mist of death to approach. Towards the light—thy last movement; an exultation of experience—thy last sound.

'Human, All-too-Human,' § 292.

PART III.

NIETZSCHE AS POET.

I. JEST, ARTIFICE, AND VENGEANCE.

(Prelude to 'The Gay Science.')

INVITATION.

Venture on my fare each feeder!
Morn will sanction such procedure,
And next day 'twill still smack good!
Then, if after more you 're thronging,
From the old store to me belonging,
Feast with me in joyous mood.

MY GOOD FORTUNE.

When I of seeking tired got,
'Twas then I learned the finding.
I 've learned, since winds against me smote,
To sail, the storms not minding.

WORLDLY WISDOM.

Stay not on a level plain!
Climb not too high above!
Most pleasure you 'll obtain,
If middle height you love.

'VADE MECUM—VADE TECUM.'

It lureth thee, my mode and speech;
Thou followest me, to hear me teach?
Nay! Guide thyself—honest and fair—
And follow me, with care! with care!

MY ROSES.

Yes! Good fortune me composes—
Yea, it always well disposes!
Would you like to cull my roses?

Ye must stoop and hide on ledges,
Oft 'twixt rocks and thorny hedges,
Wound your fingers with sharp edges!

My good fortune—likes what teases!
My good fortune—hates what pleases!
Would you like to cull those daisies?

INTERPRETATION.

Should I explain myself, I'll misexplain;
As self-expounder, therefore, I refrain.
But who his own, his proper course doth love,
Unfolds my traits in brighter light above.

THE WANDERER.

'No longer path! Abyss and silence chilling!'
So wouldst thou! From the path diverged thou willing!
Now comes the test! Keep cool, with vision clear!
Thou 'rt lost, for sure, if thou permittest fear.

THE NEIGHBOUR.

Ah! my neighbour's approximation!
Place him far off in exaltation,
As a star for my adoration!

THE DISGUISED SAINT.

That thy bliss may not distress us,
Thou assumest devils' dresses,
Devils' wit and devils' hood.
But in vain! Thy look confesses,
It proclaims thy sanctitude.

IN SUMMER.

'Twas said that in our face's sweat,
Our bread was to be eaten!
But best in sweat, bread to forget,
Is doctor's admonition.
The dog-star blinks, why should it fret?
What means its fiery twinkling?
It means that in our face's sweat,
Our wine is for our drinking.

AGAINST LAWS.

Henceforth a timepiece shall remain
About my neck, on hair-wrought chain;
Henceforth for me the starry course,
Sun, cockcrow, shadow, all lose force;
And that which ere announced the hour
Turns deaf, dumb, blind, and lacks its power;
All nature silent must withdraw,
At ticking of my watch and law.

LOSING THE HEAD.

It happened that she sense at last did find;
Because a man through her did lose his mind.
Prior to this his head had much acumen—
The devil got his head—No! no! the woman!

STAR MORALITY.

Destined, O star, for radiant path;
No claim on thee the darkness hath!

Roll on in bliss through this our age!
Its trouble ne'er shall thee engage!

In furthest worlds thy beams shall glow;
Pity, as sin, thou must not know!

Be pure: that duty's all you owe!

II. SONGS OF PRINCE FREE-AS-A-BIRD.

(Supplement to 'The Gay Science.')

TO GOETHE.

Lasting memorial
  Is thee beseeming!
God, inquisitorial,
  Is poet's bad dreaming!

World-wheel, the trundler,
  Takes many aims:
Doom—calls 't the grumbler,
  The fool calls 't—games!

World-game, impetuous,
  Blends truth and myth:
The ever fatuous
  Blends *us*—therewith!

IN THE SOUTH.

On crooked branch I 'm now a-nesting,
And cradle here my sore fatigue.
A bird invited me a-guesting;
'Tis a bird's nest wherein I 'm resting.
Where have I come? Ah, many a league!

The calm, bright sea my gaze is meeting,
A purple sail shines on the lea ;
Rock, tree, tower, port, mine eye are greeting,
Idylls around and sheep a-bleating,—
Oh, South, so guileless, harbour me !

Just step by step—that life is over ;
Leg after leg 's, like Michel, slow.
Upraised by a fair wind, the rover,
I learned it of the birds to hover,
And flew o'er seas where south winds blow.

Reason !—a matter which provokes me !
It leads too easily to one's aim !
In flying now there 's none to hoax me—
New courage, with fresh blood, evokes me
To a new life and a new game.

Lonesome to think—is not abasing,
But lonesome singing—is played out !
So hear a song to your appraising,
And sit down in a circle gazing,
Ye wanton birds all round about !

So young, false, breeze-tossed, briskly moving,
Ye seem to me just made for loving—
For all the pretty games of life ?
Up north—I do confess, unwilling—
I loved a spinster with look chilling :
'The truth '—the name of that old wife.

PIOUS BEPPA.

So long I 'm like a pearl,
  'Tis well to pious be ;
One knows God loves the girl,
  Whom pretty 'tis to see.
He will it the poor monkling
  Most certainly forgive,
That he, like many a monkling,
  So fain would with me live.

No grey church-father, greedy,
  No young, still oft a-blush,
And often, even when needy,
  With jealous wrath a-flush.
I do not love the hoary,
  He loves none old, I wis ;
How strange and wise the story
  How God arranged all this !

They have wise rules for living ;
  The church tries hearts and looks—
Me pardon ever giving,
  There 's none who me rebukes.
I lisp with mouthlet winning,
  Adieu with court'sy say,
And with the next new sinning,
  One wipes the old away.

Praise God, on earth who blesses,
  And love to maids avows,
And such-like heart distresses,
  In his own self allows.

So long I'm like a pearl,
'Tis well to pious be;
As old, disjointed girl,
Let Satan wed with me!

THE FOOL IN DESPERATION.

Ah! what I wrote on board and wall,
With foolish heart and foolish scrawl,
I meant it for their decoration.

But ye say: 'Fools' abomination,
The boards and walls, they need purgation,
That filthy lines may vanish all!'

Well! Let me help you as I can!
With sponge and broom it's my vocation,
As critic and as waterman.

But when the finished work I scan,
I see ye 'wise ones,' as most fitting,
With 'wisdom' boards and walls, besh——

SEEKING NEW SEAS.

Thither—*will* I, undismayless,
Trust myself, with sails adip,
Open lies the sea, and careless,
Saileth on my Genoa ship.

All things sparkle, new and newer,
  Noonday sleeps on time and sea;
Thine eye only, boundless viewer,
  Looks on me, infinity!

TO THE MISTRAL.

A DANCE SONG.

Mistral-Wind, thou wild cloud-chaser,
Trouble-killer, gloom-defacer,
Roarer, oh, how love I thee!
Did not the same nurture cheer us,
Firstlings of one fate, and rear us,
Preordained eternally?

Here, upon smooth rocky alleys,
How I run to meet thy sallies,
Dancing as thou pip'st and sing'st;
Who, without bark, oar, or rudder,
As the freedom's free'st brother,
Even the furious seas o'erspring'st!

Scarce awoke, through thy presaging,
Rushed I to the rocky staging,
Where the yellow sea-walls frown.
Hail! there com'st thou, like the gushing,
Diamond-sparkling streamlet, rushing
Irresistless, mountains down.

To heaven's barn-floor, eyes upturning,
Saw I thy swift horses journeying,

Saw the chariot that thee bore,
Saw thy very hands a-twitching,
As they on thy horses hitching,
Lightning-like the lashes pour;

Saw thee from thy chariot leaping,
For thy faster downward sweeping,
Saw thee, like the meteor's strake,
Plunging where the deep reposes,
As the gold rays through the roses
Of the early morning break.

Now to dance on thousand billows,
Foaming ridges, guileful pillows,—
Hail, who does *new* dance essay!
Dance we myriad steps, devoted;
Free—*our* Art shall be denoted,
And—*our* Science, be it gay!

Let us pluck from every flower
A sweet blossom for our dower,
And two leaves for wreathèd glance!
Let us dance like troubadours,
Now with saints and now with whores,
With our God and world, our dance!

He who cannot dance with breezes,
He whom swaddling-bands well pleases,
Fettered ones, lame, old, not nice—
Whatsoe'er 's like shamming Johnnies,
Titled lubbers, virtue-ponies—
Out from this our paradise!

Let us whirl the dust in doses,
Into all the sick folk's noses,
Let us scare each morbid frame,
Let us free our coast with rigour
From the breath of chests that 's meagre,
From the glance that is not game!

Let us chase the sky-obscurers,
World-blackeners, cloud-procurers,
Let us clear the realm of heaven!
Let us roar—twain with thee, free'st
Of free spirits who e'er beëst,
Roars my bliss, as if storm-driven.—

And that aye the recollection
Of such bliss have due affection,
Take this wreath with thee on high!
Toss it loftier, further, madder,
Storming up the heavenly ladder,
Hang it—on the starry sky!

III. MISCELLANEOUS PIECES.

DEDICATION to Richard Wagner and his Wife of a Copy of *Human, All-too-Human.*

T' the master and his lady fair,
Sends greetings with a joyous air,
Blessed once again with a new child,
Frederick of Basel, unbeguiled.
He seeks of them the child's inspection,
With testing hand and deep affection:
If it reveals its father's style?
Perhaps? With his moustache and smile?—
If biped-like, or all-fours walking,
'Twill make a name the world stalking?
It sought the light on mountains risky,
Like to a new-born kid turned frisky.
Whate'er the fate upon it seizing
In mundane course, it should be pleasing
To few—perhaps fifteen in all;
To others 'twill be jest and gall.
But ere it starts upon its mission,
It claims the master's benediction;
And may it follow everywhere,
The favour of his lady fair.

'Life of Nietzsche,' ii. chap. xvi.

THE TREE SPEAKS.

I 've stood too lonesome, grown too high—
I wait—but ah! for what wait I?

Too near me hangs the cloud's dark pall;
I wait for the first lightning's fall.

'Poems' (1882-85), No. 53.

THE SYBIL'S LAMENT.

Twas once—perhaps year one of our blessed
Lord—
Drunk without wine, the Sybil thus deplored:—
'How wrong things go!
Decay! Decay! Ne'er sank the world so low!
Great Rome has turned harlot and harlot-stew,
Rome's Cæsar a beast; and God has turned—
Jew!'

'Thus Spake Zarathustra,' iv.—'The Talk with the Kings.'

GREETING TO ENGLISH UTILITARIANS.

Hail! ye worthies, barrow-wheeling,
'Slowness' evermore revealing—
Stiffer aye in head and knee;
Unenraptured, never jesting,
Mediocre everlasting,
Sans génie et sans esprit!

'Beyond Good and Evil,' § 228.

SEVEN APOPHTHEGMS FOR WOMEN.

How the longest ennui flees,
When a man comes to our knees!

. . . . .

Age, alas! and science staid,
Furnish even weak virtue aid.

. . . . .

Sombre garb and silence meet,
Dresses every dame—discreet.

. . . . .

Whom I thank when in my bliss?
God! and my good tailoress!

. . . . .

Young, a flower-decked cavern home;
Old, a dragon thence doth roam.

. . . . .

Noble title, leg divine,
Man as well: Oh, were *he* mine!

. . . . .

Speech in brief and sense in mass—
Slippery for the jenny-ass!

'Beyond Good and Evil,' § 237.

ZARATHUSTRA'S ROUNDELAY.

O man! Mark well!
What saith deep midnight with its knell?
'I've slept my sleep—
And wakened from the dream's deep spell:
The world is deep,
And deeper than the day can tell.

Deep is its woe—
But joy's more deep than misery:
Woe saith: "Oh, go!"
But all joy seeks eternity—
Seeks the deep, deep eternity!'

'Thus Spake Zarathustra,' iii. and iv.

THE SIGNAL-FIRE.

Here, where 'twixt the oceans the isle has grown,
An altar-stone towering sheer aloft—
Here lit, underneath the lowering heavens,
Zarathustra his own lofty fire's blaze—
Fire-signal for castaway seamen,
Question-signal for whoe'er has an answer. . . .

The combustion with white-greyish column—
At chill remoteness licketh its desire,
To ever purer sublimeness bends its neck,
As a serpent impatiently rearing its head on high:
Lo! the signal raised for myself aloft.

For my soul itself, it is this combustion,
Insatiable for new remoteness,
Upwards, upwards, blazeth its unsullied glow.
Why fled Zarathustra from beast and mankind?
Why left he swiftly continental regions?
Six solitudes already known—
Even in the sea profoundest loneness failed him;
The isle induced to clamber, he became flame upon the mountain;

Towards a *seventh* last solitude
Casts he still in search his angle over his head.

O storm-tossed seamen! Starry dust of ages!
Ye seas of the future! Ye unexamined heavens!
To all around that 's lone, throw I now out my angle;
Give answer to my ardour's sore impatience;
Find for me—fishing on lofty mountains—
Find my seventh and *final* solitude!

'Poems' (Dionysian Dithyrambs), No. 59.

FROM LOFTY MOUNTAINS.

O noon of life! O great and solemn time!
Fair summer station!
O restless bliss in watchful expectation;
For friends I wait, both day and night sublime.
Where are ye, friends? Oh, come! 'tis time! 'tis time!

Is 't not for you to-day the glacier hoar
Bedecks with roses?
The brooklet seeks you; longing for you poses
The breeze-driven cloud now loftier than of yore—
To spy you out—where highest eagles soar.

Aloft for you my board is bounteous spread:
Whose habitation
So nigh both gulf and heavenly constellation?
My realm—whoe'er o'er wider realms did tread?
And my pure honey—whom has it ere fed?

Ye *come*, my friends! but ah, how *I* belie
Your expectation?
Ye stop, amazed—better were indignation!
I'm—he no more? Changed gait and face and eye,
No more to you the *signs* of friend imply?

Another now with my first self compared?
Aye self-outgrowing!
A wrestler many times himself o'erthrowing!
Too oft 'gainst his own force with war declared,
By his own victory wounded and impaired!

I sought the place where blew the sharpest air,
There choose my dwelling,
Where no one dwelt—those ice-bear zones repelling—
Forgetting man and God, and curse and prayer,
Became a ghost haunting the glaciers bare!

Ye friends of old, whose pallid looks so strike
With love and terror!
Go! Be not wroth! To lodge here—were an error:
Midst these far realms of ice and rocky dyke,
One must a hunter be, and chamois-like.

I'm now a hunter *vicious*! See how tight
My bow is straining;
The strongest only such a force attaining!
But ah! Dangerous is now that arrow's might,
More than all arrows! Hence! Be safe in flight! . . .

Ye go? O heart, enough thou hadst to bear,
Thy hope remaining.
Thy doors keep open now, new friends attaining!
Let go the old, nor for past memories care!
Once young—thou yet hast better youth to spare!

What ever bound us, common hopes bless'd bond—
Who reads signs pallid,
Which love once wrote thereon in symbols hallowed?
To parchment I compare it, which the hand
Unwilling grasps; it soils and makes a brand.

Thus friends, no more; they are — what name have they?
Friends, apparitions!
They haunt my door and heart for recognitions;
They look at me, 'Friends we were once,' they say:
O withered word, like fragrant rose decay!

O youthful longing, liable to stray!
Friends I desired,
Whom changed I deemed, and like to me inspired,
Advancing age has banished them away:
Who change can only 'mong my kindred stay.

O noon of life! O second youthful time!
Fair summer station!
O restless bliss in watchful expectation;
For friends I wait, both day and night sublime,
For the *new* friends! Oh, come! 'Tis time! 'tis time!

. . . .

This song is o'er—the longing's sweet refrain
Ceased with good reason,
By charmer's spell, the friend at the right season,
The noonday friend—but why should I explain—
It was at noon when one was changed to twain. . . .

We celebrate, now sure of conquering might,
The grandest lustra:
The guest of guests arrived, friend *Zarathustra*!
The world it smiled, rent was the veil of night,
The nuptials came for darkness and the light. . . .

Epode to 'Beyond Good and Evil.'

LAST WILL.

To die,
As once I saw him die—
The friend, who lightnings and glimpses
Into my gloomy youth divinely flashed:
Mischievous and deep,
In the fight a dancer,—

'Mong the warriors the cheerfulest,
'Mong the victors the gravest,
As destiny triumphing o'er his destiny,
Stern, back-seeing, foreseeing:

A-trembling *because* he had conquered,
Rapturous because that *in death* he had conquered:

Commanding, even when he died;
And his command—it was *destruction*. . . .

To die,
As once I saw him die:
Conquering, *destroying*. . . .

'Poems' (Dionysian Dithyrambs), No. 58.

PART IV.

NIETZSCHE AS PROPHET.

THUS SPAKE ZARATHUSTRA, I.

THE BEGINNING OF ZARATHUSTRA'S TEACHING.

When he was thirty years old, Zarathustra left his home and the lake by his home, and went into the mountains. There he enjoyed his spirit and the solitude, and for ten years did not weary of it. But at last his inclination changed, and rising one morning with the dawn, he went in view of the sun, and spake thus to it:—

'Thou great star! Where would be thy happiness, were it not for those whom thou illuminest?

'For ten years thou hast come up here to my cave; thou wouldst have turned sick of thy light and this route, were it not for me, my eagle, and my serpent.

'But we awaited thee every morning, relieved thee of thy superfluity, and blessed thee for it.

'Lo! I am satiated with my wisdom, like the bee that has gathered too much honey; I need hands held out.

'I would fain bestow and distribute, until the wise once more enjoy their folly, and the poor once more their riches.

'For that purpose I must descend into the deep

as thou doest in the evening, when thou goest behind the sea and givest light even to the nether world, thou exuberant star!

'Like thee I must *go down*, as men say, to whom I am about to descend.

'Bless me then, thou tranquil eye, which canst behold without envy an all-too-great happiness!

'Bless the cup that is about to overflow, that the water may flow from it in a golden stream, and carry everywhere the reflection of thy bliss!

'Lo! This cup is again going to empty, and Zarathustra is again going to be man.'

Thus began Zarathustra's exit.

When Zarathustra arrived at the nearest city adjoining the forests, he found many people assembled in the market-place; for it had been announced that a rope-dancer was to give a performance. And Zarathustra spake thus to the people:—

'*I teach you the overman.* Man is something that is to be surpassed. What have ye done to surpass man?

'All creatures hitherto have created something superior to themselves: and ye are going to be the ebb of that great tide, and would rather revert again to the beast than surpass man?

'What is the ape to man? A ridicule, or a grievous shame. And that is just what man is to be to the overman—a ridicule, or a grievous shame.

'Ye have made your way from the worm to

man, and there is still much of the worm in you. Ye were once apes, and even yet man is more of an ape than any of the apes.

'Even the wisest of you is merely a discord and hybrid of plant and spectre. But do I bid you become spectres or plants?

'Lo, I teach you the overman!

'The overman is the meaning of the earth. May your will say: the overman *shall be* the meaning of the earth.

'I conjure you my brethren, *remain true to the earth,* and do not believe those who speak to you of supernatural hopes! They are poisoners, whether they know it or not.

'They are despisers of life, decaying ones and poisoned ones themselves, of whom the earth is weary; let them begone!

'Impiety against God was once the greatest impiety; but God died, and therewith those impious ones also. To commit impiety against the earth is now the most dreadful thing, and to prize the contents of the inscrutable higher than the meaning of the earth!' . . .

When Zarathustra had thus spoken, one of the people called out: 'We have heard enough of the rope-dancer; it is now time to see him.' And all the people laughed at Zarathustra. But the rope-dancer, who thought the words applied to him, commenced his performance.

Zarathustra, however, looked at the people and was amazed. Then he spake thus:—

'Man is a connecting-rope between the animal and the overman—a rope over an abyss.

'A dangerous crossing, a dangerous wayfaring, a dangerous retrospecting, a dangerous trembling and halting.

'What is great in man is that he is a bridge and not a goal; what can be loved in man is that he is a *transit* and an *exit*.' . . .

When the morning dawned, however, Zarathustra found himself in a thick forest, and there was no longer any path visible. He then laid the dead man in a hollow tree above his head—for he wanted to protect him from the wolves—and he himself lay down on the ground and moss. And immediately he fell asleep, tired in body, but with an undisturbed soul.

Zarathustra slept long; not only did the dawn of the day pass over his head, but the forenoon as well. At last, however, his eyes opened. Zarathustra looked amazed into the forest and the stillness, he looked amazed into himself. Then he arose quickly, like a mariner discerning land all at once, and shouted for joy; for he saw a new truth. And he spake thus in his heart:—

'A light has dawned upon me: I require companions—living ones; not dead companions and corpses, which I carry with me whither I will.

'But I require living companions, who will follow me, because they want to follow themselves—to the place whither I will.

'A light has dawned upon me: Zarathustra is not to discourse to the people, but to companions! Zarathustra is not to be the herdsman and the dog of the herd! . . .

'I will associate with the creators, with the reapers, with the rejoicers; I will show them the rainbow, and all the ascents to the overman.

'I will sing my song to the lone-dwellers and to the twain-dwellers; and I will make heavy with my happiness the heart of him who has still ears for things unheard.

'I aim at my goal, I take my own course; I will leap over the loiterers and the tardy. May my course thus be their exit!'

THE THOUSAND-AND-ONE GOALS.

'Many lands did Zarathustra see, and many peoples; he thus discovered the good and bad of many peoples. No influence on earth did Zarathustra find greater than good and bad.

'No people can exist which does not first of all value things; but if a people would maintain itself, it must not value things as its neighbour values them.

'Much that was regarded as good by one people, was regarded with scorn and contempt by another; thus did I find it. I found many things called bad here, and adorned with purple honours there.

'The one neighbour never understood the

other; his soul was always amazed at his fellow's delusion and wickedness.

'A catalogue of blessings is posted up for every people. Lo! it is the catalogue of their triumphs; lo! it is the voice of their Will to Power.

'What they think difficult is laudable; what is indispensable and difficult they call good; and what relieves in the direst distress, the unique and most difficult—they extol as holy.

'Whatever enables them to rule and conquer and dazzle, to the dismay and envy of their neighbours, is regarded by them as the summit, the head, the standard, and the significance of all things.

'Verily, my brother, if thou but knewest a people's necessities, its land, its sky, and its neighbours, thou wouldst assuredy recognise the law of its ascent, and why it climbs up this ladder to its hope.

'"Thou must always be at the head and surpass the others; thy jealous soul should love no one except a friend"—that made the soul of the Greek vibrate; he thereby went on his path to greatness.

'"To speak truth and be skilful with bow and arrow"—to do so seemed alike estimable and grievous to the people from whom my name is derived—the name which is alike estimable and grievous to me.

'"To honour father and mother, and conform to their will from the very basis of the soul"—this rule for success was posted up by another people, and they became powerful and permanent thereby.

'"To be loyal, and for the sake of loyalty to risk honour and blood, even in wicked and dangerous causes"—teaching itself so, another people mastered its passions, and by thus mastering its passions, became pregnant and heavy with great hopes.

'Verily, men have made for themselves all their good and bad. Verily they did not take it, they did not find it, it did not come to them as a voice from heaven.

'Man first assigned values to things, in order to maintain himself—he first gave a significance to things, a human significance! He therefore calls himself "man," that is, the valuer.

'Valuing is creating: hear it, ye creating ones! Valuing itself is the treasure and jewel among the valued things.

'It is only through valuing that there is value; and without valuing the nut of existence is hollow. Hear it, ye creating ones!

'Change of values—that is, change of those who create. He who has to be a creator always destroys.

'Peoples were at first creators, and only in later times individuals. Verily, the individual himself is the latest creation.

'People once posted up for themselves catalogues of good things. Love which wants to rule and love which wants to obey, created such catalogues conjointly.

'The delight in the herd is older than the delight in the ego: and so long as the good conscience is the mouthpiece of the herd, the bad conscience only speaks for the ego.

'Verily, the crafty ego, the loveless ego, that seeks its advantage in the advantage of many—is not the origin of the herd, but its ruin.

'It has always been loving and creating ones that created good and bad. The fire of love glows in the names of all the virtues, and the fire of wrath.

'Many lands did Zarathustra see, and many peoples; no greater influence did Zarathustra find anywhere than the operations of the loving—they are called "good" and "bad."

'Verily, it is a prodigy, this influence of praising and blaming. Tell me, my brethren, who will restrain it for me? Who will put a fetter on the thousand necks of this animal?

'There have been a thousand goals hitherto, for there have been a thousand peoples. But the fetter for the thousand necks is still lacking: the one goal is lacking. As yet humanity is without a goal.

'But pray, tell me, my brethren: if the goal of humanity is still lacking, is not—humanity itself still lacking?'

Thus spake Zarathustra.

THE BITE OF THE ADDER.

One day, owing to the heat, Zarathustra had fallen asleep under a fig-tree, and had put his arms over his face. And there came an adder and bit him on the neck, so that he screamed with pain. When he had taken his arm from his face, he looked at the serpent; and then it recognised the eyes of Zarathustra, wriggled awkwardly, and tried to glide away. 'Not so,' said Zarathustra, 'thou hast not yet got my thanks! Thou hast awakened me in time, I have still a long journey.' 'Thou hast a short journey,' said the adder sorrowfully, 'my poison is fatal.' Zarathustra laughed. 'When did ever a dragon die of a serpent's poison?' said he. 'But take back thy poison! Thou art not rich enough to make me a present of it.' Then the adder fell on his neck once more and licked his wound.

When Zarathustra once told this story to his disciples, they asked: 'And what, O Zarathustra, is the moral of thy tale?' And with reference thereto Zarathustra answered thus:—

'The good and just call me the destroyer of morality; my tale is unmoral.

'When ye have an enemy, however, do not return him good for evil, for that would make him ashamed. But prove that he has done something good to you.

'And rather even be angry, than make a person ashamed. And when ye are cursed, it is not my pleasure that ye should desire to bless. Better curse a little also!

'And when a great injustice has been done you, do at once five more small ones! He on whom injustice presses alone is hideous to behold.

'Were ye ever aware of this? Shared injustice is half justice. And he who can bear it must take the injustice on himself!

'A small revenge is more humane than no revenge at all. And if punishment is not a right and an honour to the transgressor, I do not like your punishing.

'It is nobler to own that one is in the wrong than to carry one's point, especially when one is in the right. Only one must be opulent enough to do so.

'I do not like your cold justice; and out of the eye of your judges there always seems to me to glance the executioner and his cold steel.

'Tell me, where is justice to be found which is love with seeing eyes?

'Invent me then the love which not only bears all punishment, but also all guilt!

'Invent me then the justice which acquits every one except the judge!

'Will ye hear this likewise? To him who seeks to be just from the heart, even falsehood becomes philanthropy.

'But how could I be just from the heart! How can I give every one his own! Let this be enough for me: I give to every one my own.

'Finally, my brethren, always avoid doing wrong to the lonesome-dweller. How could a lonesome-dweller forget! How could he requite!

'A lonesome-dweller is a deep well. It is easy to throw in a stone; if it should sink to the bottom, however, tell me, who will bring it out again?

'Avoid hurting the lonesome-dweller! If, however, ye have done so, well then, kill him also!'

Thus spake Zarathustra.

ZARATHUSTRA'S FIRST RETIREMENT.

When Zarathustra had taken leave of the city to which he was devotedly attached, which bears the name 'Piebald Cow,' many people, who called themselves his disciples, followed him and kept him company. And walking thus, they came to a cross-road. Then Zarathustra told them that he wanted henceforth to go alone, for he liked being alone. At his departure, however, his disciples presented him with a staff, on the golden handle of which a serpent twined round the sun. And Zarathustra rejoiced on account of the staff; and then leaning thereon, he spake thus to his disciples:—

'Tell me, I pray you: How did gold attain to the highest value? Because it is uncommon, and unprofiting, and beaming, and soft in lustre; it always offers itself.

'Only as an image of the highest virtue did gold attain to the highest value. The countenance of the bestower beams like gold. The lustre of gold makes peace between moon and sun.

'The highest virtue is uncommon and unprofiting, it is beaming and soft of lustre; the highest virtue is a bestowing virtue.

'Verily, I divine your nature, my disciples. Ye

strive, like me, for the bestowing virtue. What would ye have in common with cats and wolves?

'It is your thirst to become sacrifices and gifts yourselves; and on that account ye have a thirst to accumulate all riches in your souls.

'Your souls strive insatiably for treasures and jewels, because your virtue is insatiable in desiring to bestow.

'Ye constrain all things to flow towards you and into you, that they may flow again from your fountainhead as the gifts of your love.

'Verily, such bestowing love must become the appropriator of all that is valuable; but I call such selfishness healthy and holy.

'There is another kind of selfishness, of a very poor and hungry nature, which would always like to steal—the selfishness of the sick, the sick selfishness.

'With the eye of the thief it looks at all that is lustrous; with the craving of hunger it takes the measure of him who has plenty to eat; and it always prowls round the tables of those who bestow.

'Sickness expresses itself in such craving, and concealed degeneration; the larcenous craving of such selfishness speaks of a sickly body.

'Tell me, my brethren, what do we regard as bad, and as the worst of things? Is it not *degeneration*?—And we always suspect degeneration when the bestowing soul is lacking.

'Our path leads upwards from the species to the over-species. But the degenerating nature which says, "All for myself," is a horror to us.' . . .

Here Zarathustra was silent for a while, and looked lovingly at his disciples. He then proceeded to speak thus, his voice being changed:—

'Remain true to the earth, my brethren, with the power of your virtue! Let your bestowing love and your knowledge be devoted to the meaning of the earth! Thus I pray and conjure you.

'Let not your virtue fly away from the earthly and beat against eternal walls with its wings! Alas, there is always so much virtue that has strayed in its flight!

'Lead back to the earth, as I do, the virtue that has strayed—yea, back again to corporeal life, that it may give to the earth its meaning—a human meaning!

'Spirit, as well as virtue, has strayed in its flight and made mistakes a hundred times hitherto. Alas, there still dwell in our body all those delusions and errors; they have there become flesh and will.

'Spirit, as well as virtue, has made trials and gone astray a hundred times hitherto. Yea, man has been an attempt. Alas, much ignorance and error has become embodied in us!

'Not only the rationality of millenniums—their madness also breaks out in us. It is dangerous to be an heir.

'We still fight step by step with the giant

chance; and irrationality, non-rationality, has hitherto ruled the whole human race.

'My brethren, let your spirit and your virtue be devoted to the meaning of the earth; let the value of everything be determined anew by you! Ye are therefore to be fighters! Ye are therefore to be creators! . . .

'There are a thousand paths which have never yet been trodden; a thousand salubrities and hidden islands of life. Man and man's world is still unexhausted and undiscovered.

'Awake and hearken, ye lonesome ones! Winds from the future arrive with stealthy flight; glad tidings are proclaimed to fine ears.

'Ye lonesome ones of the present, ye retiring ones, ye are destined one day to be a people; out of you who have chosen yourselves, a chosen people is destined to arise—and out of it the overman.

'Verily, the earth is yet destined to become a place of healing! And already a new odour is diffused over it, a salvation-bringing odour—and a new hope!'

When Zarathustra had spoken these words he was silent, like one who has not yet said his last word; he balanced the staff doubtingly in his hand for a long time. At last he spake thus, and his voice was changed:—

'I now go alone, my disciples! And ye also go away alone! I wish it to be so.

'Verily, I counsel you: depart from me, and

guard yourselves against Zarathustra! And better still: be ashamed of him! Perhaps he has deceived you.

'The man of enlightenment must be able not only to love his enemies, but to hate his friends.

'One recompenses a teacher badly when one remains always his scholar and nothing more. Why are ye unwilling to pluck at my wreath?

'Ye venerate me. But how would it be if your veneration should some day collapse? Take care less a statue crush you dead!

'Ye say, ye believe in Zarathustra? But what does it matter about Zarathustra! Ye are my believers; but what does it matter about believers!

'When as yet ye had not sought for yourselves, ye found me. So do all believers. On that account belief is always of so little importance.

'Now I bid you lose me and find yourselves; and only when ye have all denied me, will I return to you again.

'Verily, my brethren, with other eyes I shall then seek out my lost ones; I shall then love you with another love.

'And once again ye shall have become my friends and the children of one hope; then will I be with you for the third time, to celebrate the great noontide with you.

'And it is the great noontide when man is in the middle of his course between the animal and the overman, and triumphs in prospect of his path to the evening, as his highest hope; for it is the path to a new morning.

'Then, indeed, he who makes his exit will bless himself, because he is one who makes his transit; and the sun of his knowledge will be at noontide.

'*All the Gods are dead; so we now want the overman to live.* Let this be our last will at the great noontide!'

Thus spake Zarathustra.

THUS SPAKE ZARATHUSTRA, II.

THE CHILD AND THE MIRROR.

After this Zarathustra returned to the mountains and the solitude of his cave, withdrawing himself from men, and waiting like a sower who has scattered his seed. His soul, however, became impatient and full of longing for those whom he loved, for he had still much to give them. It is really the hardest thing to shut the open hand in love, and be modest as a giver.

Thus passed months and years with the lonesome one; his wisdom, however, increased, and became painful by its abundance.

But one morning he awoke ere the dawn, and having meditated long on his couch, he at last spake thus in his heart:—

'Why was I so frightened in my dream that I woke up? Did not a child come to me with a mirror?'

'"O Zarathustra" said the child to me, "look at thyself in the mirror!"

'And when I looked into the mirror I shrieked, and my heart throbbed; for it was not myself that I saw therein, but the grimace and jeering laughter of a devil.

'Verily, too well do I know the import and monition of my dream: tares pretend to be wheat!

'My enemies have grown powerful; they have distorted the form of my doctrine, so that my dearest ones involuntarily become ashamed of the gifts I gave them.

'I have lost my friends; the hour has come for me to seek those I have lost!'

With these words Zarathustra started up, not, however, like a person in anguish panting for breath, but rather like a seer and a singer whom the spirit inspires. His eagle and his serpent looked at him with amazement, for a coming bliss overspread his countenance like a rosy dawn.

'What has happened to me, ye animals?' said Zarathustra. 'Am I not transformed? Has not bliss come over me like a hurricane?

'Foolish is my happiness, and foolish things will it speak: it is too young; have patience with it.

'I am wounded with my happiness; all sufferers must be physicians to me!

'I can again go down to my friends, and also to my enemies! Zarathustra can again speak and bestow and show his best love to his dear ones.

'My impatient love overflows in streams, down towards the orient and the occident. My soul rushes into the valleys, out of silent mountains and storms of affliction.

'Too long have I yearned and gazed into the

distance. I have been too long in solitude; so I have unlearned to be silent.

'I have altogether become utterance, and the brawling of a brook among high rocks. I seek to plunge my speech into the valleys.

'And may the stream of my love sweep into pathless tracks! Why should not a stream find its way to the sea at last!

'Indeed, there is a lake in me, solitarily situated and self-contained; but the stream of my love bears it along, down—to the sea!

'I traverse new paths, a new speech comes to me; like all creators I have grown weary of the old tongues. My spirit is not going to walk any longer in worn-out shoes.

'All speech runs too slowly for me! Thou storm, I leap into thy chariot! And I will whip even thee with my waywardness!

'As a cry and a shout of joy I will skim over wide seas, till I find the Happy Isles where my friends sojourn;

'With my enemies among them! How I love every one now to whom I can merely speak! Even my enemies pertain to my bliss.

'And when I would ride my wildest horse, my spear always helps me best to mount—it is my foot's ever-ready servant;

'The spear which I hurl at my enemies. How I thank my enemies that I can at last hurl it!

'The tension of my cloud is too great: betwixt the laughters of its lightnings, I will cast hail-showers into the depth.

'Violently will my breast then heave, violently will it blow its tempest over the mountains: it will thus get relief.

'Verily, my happiness and my freedom come like a tempest! But my enemies are to believe that *the devil* roars over their heads.

'Yea, ye also, my friends, will be ashamed on account of my wild wisdom; and perhaps ye will flee from it, along with my enemies.

'Oh that I knew how to lure you back with shepherd's flutes! Oh that my lioness wisdom would learn to roar softly! And much have we learned together already!

'My wild wisdom became pregnant upon the lonesome mountains; on the rough stones it bore its young one, its youngest one.

'And now it runs wildly through the barren wilderness, and seeks and seeks for the soft sward—my old wild wisdom!

'On the soft sward of your hearts, my friends!—on your love, it would fain couch its dearest one!'

Thus spake Zarathustra.

THE PRIESTS.

And once on a time Zarathustra made a sign to his disciples and spake these words unto them:—

'Here are the priests; but though they are my enemies, pass them quietly, and with your swords at rest!

'Even among them there are heroes; many of

them have suffered too much—so they want to make others suffer.

'Bad enemies are the priests; nothing is more revengeful than their lowliness. And he who touches them easily soils himself.

'But my blood is related to theirs, and I wish withal to see my blood honoured in theirs.'—

And when they had passed, a pain attacked Zarathustra; and after struggling a little with his pain, he commenced to speak thus:—

'I deplore these priests. They are also repugnant to my taste; but that is the smallest matter to me, since I have lived among men.

'I suffer, however, and have suffered with them; they are prisoners and marked men to me. He whom they call Saviour has put them in bonds:

'In bonds of false values and illusory words! Oh that some one would save them from their Saviour!

'They once imagined they had landed on an island, when the sea tossed them hither and thither; but, behold, it was a slumbering monster!

'False values and illusory words: these are the worst monsters for mortals—long sleeps and waits the calamity in them.

'But at last its time comes, and it awakes and devours and swallows whatever has built tabernacles upon it.

'Oh, look at the tabernacles which these priests have built themselves! They call their sweet-smelling dens churches.

'Oh, their falsified light, their mustified air!

where the soul is—prevented from flying aloft to its elevation!

'But thus their belief enjoins: "On your knees, up the stairs, ye sinners!"

'Verily, I prefer to see shameless ones rather than the distorted eyes of their shame and devotion!

'Who have created for themselves such dens and penitential stairs? Was it not those who sought to conceal themselves, and were ashamed under the clear sky?

'And only when the clear sky again looks through ruined roofs, and down on the grass and red poppies on ruined walls, will I again turn my heart to the haunts of this God.

'They called God what opposed and afflicted them; and verily there was much heroic spirit in their worship.

'And they knew not how to love their God otherwise than by nailing men to the cross!

'They sought to live as corpses, they draped their corpses in black; even in their talk I still trace the sickening odour of charnel-houses.

'And he who lives nigh to them, lives nigh to black pools, in which the toad sings its song with sweet melancholy.

'They must sing better songs for me to learn to believe in their Saviour; his disciples must seem more saved-like for me!

'I should like to see them naked, for beauty alone ought to preach penitence. But whom will their disguised affliction convince!

'Verily, their Saviours themselves did not come from freedom and freedom's seventh heaven! Verily, they themselves never trod on the carpets of knowledge!

'The spirit of these Saviours was made up of defects; but into every defect they had put their illusion, their stop-gap, which they called God.

'Their own spirit was drowned in sympathy; and when they swelled and swelled therewith, a great folly always floated on the surface.

'Eagerly and with shouts they drove the flock over their plank-bridge, as if there were only one plank-bridge to the future! Verily, these shepherds still belonged to the sheep.

'Poor spirits and bulky souls had these shepherds; but, my brethren, what poor soil have even the most bulky souls been!

'Characters of blood were written by them on their path, and in their folly they thought truth was proved by blood.

'But blood is the worst of all witnesses for truth; blood poisons even the purest teaching, and turns it into delusion and hatred of heart.

'And when a man goes through fire for his teaching—what does it prove? Verily, rather that his own teaching cometh from his own burning.

'A sultry heart and a cold head: when these meet, there arises the blusterer, the "Saviour."

'Verily there have been greater ones and higher-born than the overpowering blusterers whom the people call Saviours.

'And by still greater ones than any of the Saviours must ye be saved, my brethren, if ye would find the way to freedom!

'Never yet has there been an overman. I have seen both naked, the greatest man and the smallest man:

'They are still all-too-similar to each other. Verily, I found even the greatest—all-too-human!'

Thus spake Zarathustra.

THE WILL TO POWER.

'Hearken now to my word, ye wisest ones! Test it seriously if I have crept into the heart of life itself, and into the roots of its heart!

'Wherever I found a living being I found the Will to Power, and even in the will of him who serves I found the will to be master.

'That the weaker should serve the stronger—that is what he persuadeth his will, who wants to be master over what is still weaker. That delight alone a living being does not like to forego.

'And as the smaller surrenders itself to the greater, that it may have delight and power with respect to what is smallest of all, so the greatest even surrenders itself, and for the sake of power, stakes—life.

'It is the surrendering of the greatest to run risk and danger, and cast dice for death.

'And wherever there is sacrifice and service and looks of love, there, also, is the will to be master.

The weaker accordingly slinks into the fortress by backways, and even into the heart of the mightier one—and steals his power.

'This secret—life itself uttered to me. "Behold," it said, "I am that *which must ever surmount itself.*

'"To be sure, ye call it will to procreate, or impulse towards its purpose, towards the higher, the more remote, the more manifold; but all that is one and the same secret.

'"Rather would I succumb than disown this one thing; and verily, where there is succumbing and leaf falling, lo! life sacrifices itself there for power!

'"That I have to be struggle, and becoming, and purpose, and cross-purpose—ah, he who divines my will, divines surely on what crooked paths it has to tread.

'"Whatever I create, and however much I love it—I have soon to be hostile to it, and to my love: so my will determines.

'"And even thou, knowing one, art merely the path and the footsteps of my will: verily, my Will to Power walks also on the feet of thy will to truth.

'"He, assuredly, did not hit the truth who shot at it the formula, "Will to Existence." There is no such will.

'"For that which does not exist cannot exercise will; that which is in existence, however, how could it exercise will to existence?

'"Only where there is life there is will; not, however, Will to Life, but—such is my teaching—Will to Power!

'"Much is more highly prized by the living being than life itself, but out of that very appraisement speaks—the Will to Power!"

'Thus did life teach me once on a time; and therewith, ye wisest ones, I solve you the riddle of your hearts.'

THE LAND OF CULTURE.

'Too far did I fly into the future; a horror seized upon me.

'And when I looked around, lo! time was my only contemporary there.

'Then I flew backward, homeward—and always faster. I thus came to you, ye present-day men, and into the land of culture.

'For the first time I brought eyes to discern you, and desire to do so. Verily, I came with longing in my heart.

'But how did it happen to me? Though I was so alarmed—I had yet to laugh! Never did my eyes behold anything so motley-coloured!

'I laughed and laughed, while my foot still trembled, and my heart likewise. "Here, indeed, is the home of all the paint-pots," I said.

'With fifty patches painted on your faces and limbs—ye sat there to my astonishment, ye present-day men!

'And with fifty mirrors around you, which flattered your play of colours, and spake well of it!

'Verily, ye could not possibly wear better

masks, ye present-day men, than your own faces are! Who could—*know* you!

'Written all over with the characters of the past, and these characters also daubed over with new characters—ye have thus hidden yourselves well from all diviners.

'And even if one should be a trier of the reins, who could ever believe that ye have reins! Ye seem to be baked out of colours and glued scraps.

'All times and peoples gaze motley-coloured out of your veils; all customs and beliefs speak motley-coloured out of your gestures.

'He who would strip you of veils and wrappers, and paint and gestures, would just have enough left to scare the crows.

'Verily, I myself am the scared crow who once saw you naked and without paint; and I flew away when the skeleton ogled at me.

'I would rather be a day-labourer in the nether-world, and among the shadows of the bygone! Those in the nether-world are certainly fatter and fairer than ye!

'This, yea this, is bitterness to my bowels, that I can neither endure you naked nor clothed, ye present day men!

'All that is dismal in the future, and whatever makes strayed birds shudder, is verily more home-like and familiar than your "reality."

'For ye say: "We are wholly real and without belief and superstition": thus ye set yourselves up proudly—ah, even without breasts!

'Indeed, how *could* ye possibly believe, ye

motley-coloured ones!—ye who are the pictures of all that has ever been believed!

'Ye are yourselves perambulating refutations of beliefs and breakages of the links of universal thought. *Men unworthy of belief:* thus *I* call you, ye real ones.

'All periods prate against one another in your spirits; yet the dreams and pratings of all periods were more real than your awakeness!

'Ye are unproductive; *therefore* ye lack belief. He, however, who had to create, had always also his presaging dreams and astral premonitions—and believed in belief!—

'Ye are half-open doors at which grave-diggers wait. And this is *your* reality: "Everything is worthy to perish."

'Ah, how ye stand there, ye unproductive ones, how lean your ribs! And many of you have even had cognisance thereof.

'Many a one has said: "Surely a God has filched something from me stealthily while I slept? Verily, enough to make a girl for himself out of!

'"The poverty of my ribs is amazing": many a present-day man has spoken thus.

'Yea, ye are a laughter to me, ye present-day men! And especially when ye are surprised at yourselves!

'And woe to me if I could not laugh at your surprise, and had to gulp down all that is repugnant in your basins!

'As it is, I will make lighter of you, since I have

to carry ***what is heavy***; and what does it matter to me if beetles and winged grubs should alight on my load?

'Verily, it shall not on that account become heavier to me! And not from you, ye present-day men, shall my great weariness result.—

'Ah, where am I now to ascend with my longing! From all mountains I look out towards father-lands and mother-lands.

'But I have found a home nowhere; wandering about, I am in all cities, and decamping from all gates.

'Alien to me, and a mockery to me are the present-day men, to whom my heart lately impelled me; and I am exiled from father-lands and mother-lands.

'Thus I still love only my ***children's land,*** the undiscovered in the most distant seas; I enjoin on my sails to search and search for it.

'To my children will I make amends for being the child of my fathers, and to all the future—for ***this*** present day.'

Thus spake Zarathustra.

ZARATHUSTRA AND THE HUNCHBACK.

One day when Zarathustra went over the great bridge, the cripples and beggars surrounded him, and a hunchback spake thus to him:—

'Lo, Zarathustra! The people also learn from thee and acquire belief in thy teaching; but, that they may fully believe in thee, one thing is still needful — thou must first of all convince us cripples! Here thou hast now a fine selection, and verily an opportunity with more than one forelock! Thou canst heal the blind and make the lame run; and for him who has too much behind, thou couldst also perhaps abstract a little. That would be the right way, I think, to make the cripples believe in Zarathustra!'

But Zarathustra answered thus to him who so spake:—'When one takes his hump from the hunchback, one takes from him his spirit—so say the people. And when one gives eyes to the blind man, he sees too many bad things on the earth, so much so, that he curses him who healed him. But he who makes the lame man run, inflicts on him the greatest injury, for no sooner can he run, than his vices run away with him--so say the people concerning cripples. And why should not Zarathustra also learn from the people, when the people learn from Zarathustra?

'It is, however, of the smallest consequence to me, since I have been among men, to see one person lacking an eye, another an ear, and a third a leg; and that there are others who have lost the tongue, or the nose, or the head.

'I see, and have seen worse than any of these—yea, divers things so hideous, that I should neither like to speak of all I have seen, nor even to keep silent about some matters; namely, men who lack everything, except that they have too much of one thing—men who are nothing more than a big eye, or a big mouth, or a big belly, or something else big. I call such men reversed cripples.

'And when I came out of my solitude and passed over this bridge for the first time, I could not trust my eyes, but looked again and again, and said finally: "That is an ear! an ear as big as a man!" I look still more attentively—and actually there did move under the ear something that was pitiably small and poor and slim. And, in truth, the immense ear was borne by a small, thin stalk—the stalk, however, was the man! A person putting a glass to his eyes could even recognise a small, envious countenance, and that a bloated little soul dangled at the stalk. The people told me, however, that the big ear was not only a man, but a great man, a genius. But I never believe in the people when they speak of great men—and I hold on to my belief that it was a reversed cripple, who had too little of all else and too much of one thing.'

When Zarathustra had spoken thus to the hunchback, and to those of whom the hunchback was the mouthpiece and advocate, he turned to his disciples in profound dejection, and said:—

'Verily, my friends, I walk among men as among the fragments and members of human beings!

'This is the terrible thing to me, that I find man broken up and scattered about, as over a battle- and butcher-field.

'And when my eye flees from the present to the bygone, it finds ever the same: fragments and members and dismaying chances—but no men!

'The present and the bygone on earth—ah! my friends—that is the most unendurable to *me*; and I should not know how to live, if I were not a seer of things to come.

'A seer, a purposer, a creator, a future itself and a bridge to the future—and ah! still as it were a cripple on this bridge: all that is Zarathustra.

'And ye also ask yourselves often: "Who is Zarathustra to us? What shall he be called by us?" And like myself, ye gave yourselves questions for answers.

'Is he a promiser? Or a fulfiller? A capturer? Or an inheritor? A harvest? Or a ploughshare? A physician? Or a healed one?

'Is he a poet? Or a genuine one? An emancipator? Or a subjugator? A good or an evil one?

'I walk among men as among the fragments of the future, of the future which I see.

'And this is all my poetisation and aspiration—to compose and unify what is fragment and riddle and dismaying chance.

'And how could I endure to be man, if man were not also a composer and riddle-reader and redeemer of chance!

'To redeem the past, and to transform every "It was" into "Thus I willed it!"—that only do I call redemption!

'Will—so the emancipator and joy-bringer is called. Thus have I taught you, my friends.'

THUS SPAKE ZARATHUSTRA, III.

THE WANDERER.

When it was about midnight, Zarathustra went his way over the ridge of the isle, so as to arrive early in the morning at the other seacoast; for there he wanted to go on board ship. There was, in fact, a good roadstead there, in which even foreign ships liked to anchor. These ships took many people with them, who wanted to cross the sea from the Happy Isles. When therefore Zarathustra ascended the mountain, he thought during the way of his many solitary wanderings from youth onwards, and how many mountains and ridges and summits he had already climbed.

'I am a wanderer and mountain-climber,' he said in his heart; 'I do not love the plains, and it seems I cannot long sit still.

'And whatever may yet come to me as fate and experience, there will be wandering therein and mountain-climbing; in the end one experiences only one's true self.

'The time is gone by when chances could happen to me; what *could* now fall to my lot, not already my own

'It merely returns, it comes home to me at

last—my own self, and such of it as has been long abroad and scattered wide among things and chances.

'And one thing more I know: I now stand before my last summit, and before that which has been longest reserved for me. Ah, I must climb up my most difficult path! Ah, I have begun my most lonely wandering!

'He who is of my nature, however, does not escape such an hour; the hour that says to him: "Now for the first time thou goest the way of thy greatness! Summit and abyss—these are now consummated in one!

'"Thou goest the way of thy greatness; what has hitherto been called thy final danger has now become thy final refuge!

'"Thou goest the way of thy greatness. This must now be thy best courage, that there is no longer any path behind thee!

'"Thou goest the way of thy greatness. No one shall steal after thee! Thy foot itself has extinguished the path behind thee, and over it there stands written: "Impossibility."

'"And if all ladders are now lacking, thou must be able to climb on thy own head; how couldst thou climb upwards otherwise?

'"On thy own head and beyond thy own heart! The softest in thee must now become the hardest.

'"He who has always indulged himself sickens at last by his over-indulgence. Praises on that which makes hardy! I do not praise the land where butter and honey—flow!

'"One has to learn *to leave oneself out of account* in order to see *many things*: this hardiness is required by every mountain climber.

'"He, however, who is obtrusive with his eyes as a diagnoser, how could he see more than the foreground of things!

'"But thou, O Zarathustra, wouldst view the heart of things and their background; so thou must climb beyond thyself—upwards, up, until thou hast even the stars *under* thee!"

'Yea! To see down on myself, and even on my stars: that only would I call my *summit*, that has remained for me as my *last* summit!'

Thus spake Zarathustra to himself while climbing, comforting his heart with stern maxims; for he was sore troubled as he had never been before. And when he came to the top of the mountain-ridge, behold, there lay the other sea stretched out before him, and he stood still and was long silent. The night, however, was cold at that elevation, and clear, with bright starlight.

'I am sensible of my destiny,' he said at last, mournfully. 'Very well! I am ready. My last lonesomeness has just begun.

'Ah, this black, mournful sea below me! Ah, this pregnant, nocturnal listlessness! Ah, fate and sea! To you I have now to go *down*!

'I stand before my highest mountain and before my longest wandering; I have first, therefore, to go deeper down than ever I ascended;

'Deeper down into pain than I ever ascended —even into the blackest flood! So my fate wills it! Very well! I am ready.

'"Whence come the highest mountains?" I asked once. I then learned that they came out of the sea.

'That testimony is inscribed on their stones, and on the walls of their summits. The highest has to come to its height out of the deepest.'

Thus spake Zarathustra on the top of the mountain where it was cold; when, however, he came to the vicinity of the sea, and stood alone at last among the cliffs, he had become weary of the way, and more ardent in longing than before.

'Everything sleeps as yet,' he said, 'even the sea sleeps; its eye looks at me drowsily and unfamiliarly.

'But it breathes warmly—I feel that. And I feel also that it dreams. Dreaming, it tosses about on hard pillows.

'Hark! Hark! How it groans with evil recollections! Or evil expectations?

'Ah, I am sorrowful along with thee, thou dusky monster, and I am angry with myself even on that account.'

'Alas, that my hand has not strength enough! Gladly, indeed, would I deliver thee from evil dreams!'

And while thus speaking, Zarathustra laughed at himself with melancholy and bitterness. 'What! Zarathustra,' said he, 'wilt thou even sing consolation to the sea?

'Ah, thou amiable fool, Zarathustra, thou over-credulous one. But thou wast always so; thou always venturedst confidently to what was terrible.

'Thou wouldst even caress a monster. A sniff of warm breath, a little soft tuft on the claw—and at once thou art ready to love and allure it.

'Love is the danger of the lonesome, the love to everything, *if it only lives*! It is verily ludicrous, my folly and modesty in love!'

Thus spake Zarathustra, and laughed therewith a second time. Then, however, he thought of his forsaken friends; and as if he had done them a wrong with his thoughts, he was angry with himself on account of his thoughts. And forthwith it came to pass that the laugher wept; with anger and longing Zarathustra wept bitterly.

THE VISION AND THE ENIGMA.

When it became known among the crew that Zarathustra was on board the ship—for a man who came from the Happy Isles had gone on board with him—there was great curiosity and expectation. But Zarathustra kept silent for two days, and was cold and deaf with sadness, so that he neither answered looks nor questions. On the evening of the second day, however, he again opened his ears, although he still kept silent; for there was much to be heard of what was curious and dangerous on board the ship, which came from afar and meant to go still further. And Zarathustra was fond of all those who made distant voyages, and are not anxious to be free from danger. And behold! his own tongue at last became loosed, and the ice of his heart broke. He then began to speak thus:—

'To you the daring attempters and tempters, and whoever embarks with cunning sails on terrible seas—

'To you, the enigma-intoxicated, the twilight-lovers, whose souls are allured by flutes to every treacherous gulf—

'For ye will not grope after a thread with cowardly hand; and where ye can *divine*, ye hate to *deduce*—

'To you only do I tell the enigma that I saw—the vision of the lonesomest one.

'Gloomy, I walked recently in corpse-coloured twilight—gloomy and stern, with compressed lips. Not one sun only had set for me.

'A path which ascended daringly among boulders, a weird lonesome path which neither herb nor bush any longer cheered, a mountain path crunched under the daring of my foot.

'Stepping mutely over the scornful clinking of the pebbles, trampling the stone that let it slip: thus my foot forced its way upwards.

'Upwards—in spite of the spirit which drew it downwards, abysm-wards, the spirit of heaviness, my devil and arch-enemy.

'Upwards—although it sat on me, half-devil,

half-mole; halt, paralysing, dripping lead through my ears, and lead-drop thoughts into my brain.

'"O Zarathustra," it whispered scornfully, syllable by syllable, "thou stone of wisdom! Thou threwest thyself high, but every thrown stone must—fall!

'"O Zarathustra, thou stone of wisdom, thou sling-stone, thou star-destroyer! Thou threwest thyself so high, but every thrown stone—must fall!

'"Condemned to self-punishing, and to thy own stoning! O Zarathustra, thou indeed threwest thy stone far—but it will fall back on *thyself*!"

'Thereupon the dwarf kept silence, which continued for a long time. Its silence, however, oppressed me; and for two to be in such a case, it is verily more lonesome than for one!

'I ascended, I dreamed, I thought—but everything oppressed me. I was like a sick person whose dreadful torture makes him weary, and whose more dreadful dream re-awakes him when falling asleep.

'But there is something in me which I call courage; it had hitherto slain every dejection in me. That courage at last commanded me to stand still and say, "Dwarf! Thou! Or I!"

'For courage is the best slayer—courage which attacks; for every attack is a stirring game.

'Man is the most courageous animal; he thereby overcame every other animal. In the stirring game he has even overcome every pain; human pain, however, is the sorest pain.

'Courage also slays giddiness at abysses; and where is man not confronted with abysses! Is not seeing itself, seeing abysses?

'Courage is the best slayer; courage also slays fellow-suffering. Fellow-suffering, however, is the deepest abyss; as deeply as man looks into life, so deeply also does he look into suffering.

'Courage, however, is the best slayer, courage which attacks; it slays even death; for it says, "Was *that* life? Well! Once more!"

'In such a saying, however, there is much of the stirring game. He who hath ears to hear, let him hear.'

'"Halt! dwarf," said I, "either thou or I! I am, however, the stronger of the two. Thou art unaware of my abysmal thought! Thou couldst not endure *it*!"

'Then there happened that which made me feel less oppressed; for the dwarf, the inquisitive creature, jumped from my shoulder! And it squatted on a stone in front of me.

'There was, however, a gateway just where we halted.

'"Look at this gateway, dwarf," I continued, "it has two faces. Two paths meet here; no one ever went to the end of either.

'"This long lane behind goes on for an eternity. And that long lane outward—it goes on for another eternity.

'"They are antithetical, these two paths; they run right against each other; and it is here at this gateway that they meet. The name of the gateway is inscribed above: The Present Moment.

'"And if a person should follow one of these paths further—and ever further and further on, thinkest thou, dwarf, that these paths would be eternally antithetical?"

'"Everything straight lies," murmured the dwarf contemptuously, "truth is all crooked, time itself is a circle."

'"Thou spirit of heaviness," said I wrathfully, "do not take it too lightly! Or I shall leave thee to squat there so low, lame-leg!—and I carried thee so high!

'"Consider," continued I, "this Present Moment. From this gateway, The Present Moment, there runs a long, eternal lane backwards; behind us lies an eternity.

'"Must not whatever *could* run its course, of all things, have already run along that lane? Must not whatever *could* happen have happened, gone by, and been accomplished already?

'"And if everything has already been there, what thinkest thou, dwarf, of this Present Moment? Must not even this gateway have already been there?

'"And are not all things closely bound together in such wise that this Present Moment draws everything in the future after it. *Therefore*—itself likewise?

'"For whatever can run its course of all things, along that long lane—*must* it once more run.

'"And this slow spider which creeps in the

moonlight, and this moonlight itself, and thou and I whispering together in this gateway—whispering of eternal things—must we not all have been there before?

'"And must we not return and run in that other lane before us, that long, awful lane? Must we not return eternally?"

'This I spake in ever-softening tones; for I was afraid of my own thoughts and the suggestions of my heart. Then suddenly I heard a dog *howl* close at hand.

'Did I ever hear a dog howl thus? My thoughts ran back. Yes! when I was a child, in my most distant childhood;

'Then I heard a dog howl thus. And saw it also, its hair ruffled, its head turned upwards, trembling in the stillest midnight, when even dogs believe in ghosts;

'So that it moved me to pity. For just then the full moon, silent as death, passed over the house; just then it stood still, a round glare—at rest on the flat roof, as if on other people's property:

'On that account the dog had been terrified; for dogs believe in thieves and ghosts. And when I again heard a howling like that, it moved me to pity once more.

'Where had the dwarf gone? And the gateway? And the spider? And all the whispering? Had I dreamt? Had I waked up? All at once I stood among wild cliffs, alone, solitary, in the most solitary moonlight.

'*But there lay a man!* And there! The dog leaping, ruffled, whining—it now saw me coming —it then howled again, and *cried*: did I ever hear a dog cry for help in such a way?

'And verily, what I saw, the like of it I had never seen. I saw a young shepherd writhing, choking, quivering, with distorted countenance, with a black, heavy serpent hanging out of his mouth.

'Did I ever see so much loathsomeness and pale horror on one countenance? He had probably slept? Then the serpent had crawled into his throat—there it took firm hold with its mouth.

'My hand pulled at the serpent and pulled—in vain! It could not pull the serpent out of his throat. Then there cried out of me: "Bite! bite!—

'"Its head off! Bite!"—so it cried out of me; my horror, my hate, my loathing, my pity, all my good and bad cried with one cry out of me.

'Ye daring ones around me! Ye attempters and tempters, and whoever of you embark with cunning sails on unexplored seas! Ye rejoicers in enigmas!

'Just solve for me the enigma which I then looked on; interpret to me the vision of the lonesomest one!

'For it was a vision and a foresight: *what* did I then behold in simile? And *who* is it that has to come some day?

'*Who* is the shepherd into whose throat the serpent thus crawled? Who is the man into whose throat all the heaviest and blackest will thus crawl?

'The shepherd, however, bit, as my cry admonished him; he bit with a powerful bite! Far away he spat the head of the serpent—and sprang up.

'No longer shepherd, no longer man—a transfigured being, that *laughed*! Never on earth had a man laughed as *he* laughed.

'Oh, my brethren, I heard a laughter which was no human laughter—and now a thirst gnaws at me, a longing which is never allayed.

'My longing for that laughter gnaws at me! Oh, how do I yet endure to live! And how could I endure it to die at present!'

Thus spake Zarathustra.

THE OLD AND NEW TABLES.

'Here I sit and wait, old broken tables around me, and also new, half-written tables. When will my hour arrive?—

'The hour of my descent, of my downgoing? —For I must go once more to man.

'For that hour I now wait; for the signs have first to come to me that it is *my* hour—namely, the laughing lion, with the flock of doves.

'Meanwhile, I speak to myself as one who has sufficient time. No one tells me anything new, so I tell myself my own story.

'When I came to men, I found them living under an old infatuation; they all thought they had long known what was good and bad.

'All discourse about virtue seemed to them an old wearisome business; and he who wished to sleep well, spake of "good" and "bad" before retiring to rest.

'This somnolence I disturbed when I taught that *no one yet knows* what is good and bad—unless it be he who creates!

'It is he, however, who furnishes man's goal, and gives to the earth its meaning and its future; he only brings it about that things are good and bad.

'And I enjoined them to overturn their old academic chairs, and wherever that old infatuation had sat; I enjoined them to laugh at their great moralists, their saints, their poets, and their saviours.

'At their gloomy wise ones I enjoined them to laugh, and at whatever had sat admonishing, as a black scarecrow, on the tree of life.

'Beside their great row of graves I seated myself, and even with the carrion and vultures; and I laughed at all their bygone, with its mellow, decaying glory.

'Verily, like penitential preachers and fools, I cried wrath and shame on all their greatness and smallness. Oh that their best is so very small! Oh that their worst is so very small!—thus did I laugh.

'Thus did my wise longing, which has its birthplace in the mountains, cry and laugh in me, a wild wisdom, verily!—my great, pinion-flapping longing.

'And oft in the midst of laughing it hurried me aloft and away; then I would fly, quivering like an arrow, with sun-intoxicated rapture,

'Out into distant futures, which no dream has yet seen, into warmer souths than ever sculptor conceived, where Gods in their dancing are ashamed of all clothes.

'Behold, here is a new table; but where are my brethren who will carry it with me to the valley and into the hearts of flesh?—

'Thus does my great love to the remotest ones demand: "*Disregard thy neighbours*! Man is something that is to be surpassed."

'There are many divers ways and modes of surpassing; see *thou* thereto! But only a buffoon thinks that man can be *overleapt* also.

'Surpass thyself even through thy neighbour; and a right which thou canst seize upon, shalt thou not allow to be given thee!

'What thou doest, no one can do it to thee again; lo, there is no indemnification!

'He who cannot command himself shall obey. And many a one *can* command himself, but still sorely lacks self-obedience.

'To be true—few can be so! And those who can are unwilling. But least of all can the good be true.

'Oh, those good people! *Good men never speak the truth;* to be good in such a manner is an infirmity of the mind.

'They give in, those good people, they give themselves up; their heart repeats, their reason obeys: he, however, who obeys, *does not listen to himself*!

'All that the good call evil must come together for one truth to be born. Oh, my brethren, are ye evil enough for *this* truth?

'The daring attempt, the prolonged mistrust, the cruel Nay, the tedium, the cutting into the quick—how seldom do *these* come together! Out of such seed, however, truth is produced!

'*Alongside of* the bad conscience, all *knowledge* has hitherto grown! Break up, ye knowing ones, break up the old tables!

'There is an old illusion called good and evil. Around soothsayers and astrologers the orbit of this illusion has hitherto revolved.

'Once one *believed* in soothsayers and astrologers; and *therefore* one believed: "All is fate; thou oughtest, for thou must!"

'Then again, one distrusted all soothsayers and astrologers, and *therefore* one believed: "All is freedom; thou canst, for thou willest!"

'Oh, my brethren, concerning the stars and the future there has hitherto been only illusion, and not knowledge; and *therefore* concerning good and evil there has hitherto been only illusion and not knowledge!'

'"Thou shalt not rob!" "Thou shalt not slay!"—such precepts were once called holy;

people bowed their heads and their knees before them, and took off their shoes.

'But I ask you, where were there ever worse robbers and slayers than these holy precepts?

'Is there not robbery and slaying in all forms of life? And for such precepts to be called holy, was not the *truth* itself thereby—slain?

'Or was it the preaching of death to call holy that which contradicts and dissuades from life?—Oh, my brethren, break up, I pray you, break up the old tables!'

'Oh, my brethren, I consecrate and point you the way to a new nobility; ye are to be the procreators, the cultivators, and the sowers of the future.

'Verily, not a nobility which ye could purchase like traders with traders' gold; for all that has its price is of little value.

'Let it not be your honour henceforth whence ye come, but whither ye go! Your will and your feet which aspire to surpass you—let these be your new honour!

'Verily, not that ye have served a prince—of what account are princes now!—nor that ye have become a bulwark to what is established, that it may stand more securely.

'Not that your family has become courtly at courts, and that, gay-coloured like the flamingo, ye have learned to stand long hours in shallow pools.

('For ability to stand is a merit among courtiers;

and all courtiers believe that *permission* to sit pertains to blessedness after death !)

'Nor even that a Spirit called Holy led your forefathers into a land which *I* do not praise (for where the cross, the worst of all trees, grew—in that land there is nothing to praise !

'And, verily, wherever this Holy Spirit led its knights, in such campaigns, goats and geese, and crossheads and wrongheads always ran on *before* !)

'Oh, my brethren, it is not backward that your nobility must gaze, but *outward* ! Ye have to be exiles from all father-lands and forefather-lands !

'Ye must love your *children's land* (let that love be your new nobility), the undiscovered in the most distant sea ! I enjoin you to search for it with your sails !

'To your children ye must *make amends* for being the children of your fathers : ye have *thus* to redeem all the past ! This new table I put up for you !'

'Here are maxims which I have heard pious backworld's-men utter to their consciences, and verily without wickedness or deceit—although there is nothing more deceitful and wicked :—

'"Let the world take care of itself ! Do not raise a finger against it !

'"Whoever is inclined, let him strangle and stab and cut and scratch the people ; do not raise a finger against it ! They will thereby learn to renounce the world.

'"And thine own reason—thou thyself must choke and strangle it; for it is reason of the world. Thou thyself wilt thereby learn to renounce the world."—

'Break up, my brethren, break up those old tables of the pious! Disparage altogether the maxims of the calumniators of the world!'

'"He who learns much unlearns all violent cravings"—that is what people now whisper to themselves in all the dark streets.

'"Wisdom makes one weary, nothing is worth while; thou shalt not crave!"—this new table I found put up even in the open markets.

'Break up, I pray you, break up that *new* table also! The weary-o'-the-world put it up, the preachers of death and the jailers; for lo! it is also a homily of slavery.'

'Ye are only to have enemies to be hated, not enemies to be despised. Ye must be proud of your enemies.

'For the worthiest enemies, my friends, ye are to reserve yourselves; ye must therefore pass many a one by.

'Go *your own* ways! and let the people and peoples go theirs!—gloomy ways certainly, on which not even a single hope glints any more!

'Let the trader rule where all that still shines is traders' gold! It is the era of kings no longer: that which at present calls itself the people is unworthy of kings.

'See how the people themselves now do just as the traders; they pick up the smallest advantage, even out of the rubbish!

'They lie in wait for one another, they obtain a little from one another by lurking stealthily—they call that "good neighbourliness." Oh, blessed, remote period, when a people said to itself: "We mean to be *masters* over peoples!"

'For, my brethren, the best shall rule, the best also mean to rule! And where a different doctrine prevails, there the best things are lacking.'

'Thus would I have man and woman: the one fit for war, the other fit for child-bearing; both of them, however, fit for dancing with head and limbs.

'And may the day be lost to us in which a measure has not been danced! And may every truth be called false which has not been accompanied with laughter!'

'He who has grown wise concerning old origins, lo, he will ultimately seek after the fountains of the future, and new origins.

'Oh, my brethren, it will not be long until new peoples arise and new fountains rush down into new depths.

'The earthquake, as one knows, chokes many wells, and causes much languishing; but it brings also to light inner powers and secrets.

'The earthquake discloses new fountains. In the earthquake of the old peoples new fountains burst forth.

'And he who then calls out: "Lo, here is a well for many thirsty ones, a heart for many longing ones, a will for many instruments," around him there collects a *people*, that is, many essaying ones.

'Who can command, who must obey?—*that is what is essayed there!* Ah, with what long seeking, and solving, and failing, and learning, and reattempting!

'Human society: it is an attempt—so I teach—a long seeking; it seeks, however, the ruling one!

'An attempt, my brethren! And no "contract"! Destroy, I pray you, destroy such slang of the soft-hearted and the half-and-half!'

'Oh, my brethren, with whom lies the greatest danger to the human future? Is it not with the good and just?

'As being those who say and feel in their hearts: "We already know what is good and just, we possess it also; woe to those who still seek for it!"

'And whatever harm the wicked may do, the harm of the good is the worst harm!

'And whatever harm the world-maligners may do, the harm of the good is the worst harm!

'Oh, my brethren, once on a time there was one who saw into the hearts of the good and just, and said, "They are Pharisees." But people did not understand him.

'The good and just themselves were not at liberty to understand him; their intellect was in the power of their good conscience. The stupidity of the good is profoundly wise.

'It is the truth, however, that the good *must* be Pharisees—they have no choice!

'The good *must* crucify him who devises his own virtue! That is the truth!

'The second one, however, who discovered their land—the land, heart, and soil of the good and just—was he who asked: "Whom do they hate most?"

'They hate the *creating* one most, him who breaks the tables and old standard values, the breaker—they call him the law-breaker.

'The good, as one knows, they *cannot* create; they are always the beginning of the end;

'They crucify him who inscribes new standard values on new tables, they sacrifice the future *to themselves*, they crucify the whole future of man!

'The good—they have always been the beginning of the end.'

'Oh, my brethren, when I enjoined on you to destroy the good, and the tables of the good, then only did I embark man on his high seas.

'And now only does the great terror come to him, the great outlook, the great illness, the great nausea, the great sea-sickness.

'The good taught you concerning false coasts and false securities; in the lies of the good ye were born and kept blind. Everything has been radically falsified and stultified by the good.

'But he who discovered the land of "man" discovered also the land of "man's future." Ye have now to be seafarers for me, brave and patient!

'Keep yourselves up, my brethren, learn to keep yourselves up! The sea is violent. Many seek to re-arise by your aid.

'The sea is violent; all is in the sea. Well! Cheer up! Ye old seaman hearts!

'What fatherland! Our helm urges us *thitherwards* where our *children's land* is! Thitherwards, more violently than the sea, surges our great longing!'

THE ETERNAL RETURN.

One morning, not long after returning to his cave, Zarathustra sprang up from his couch like a person frantic, crying with a frightful voice, and making gestures, as if some one still lay on the couch who did not wish to rise; his voice, moreover, resounded in such a manner that his animals came to him frightened, and the creatures in the neighbouring caves and lurking-places slipped away, each of them flying, fluttering, creeping, or leaping, according to the variety of foot or wing with which it was furnished. Zarathustra, however, spake these words:—

'Up, abysmal thought, out of my depth! I am thy cock and morning-dawn, thou drowsy worm. Up! Up! My voice shall soon crow thee awake!

'Loosen the fetters of thy ears! Listen! I

want to hear thee! Up! Up! There is thunder enough to make the very graves listen!

'Rub the sleep and all the dimness and blindness out of thine eyes! Hear me also with thine eyes: my voice is a medicine even for those born blind.

'And once thou art awake I will keep thee always awake. It is not *my* custom to awake great-grandmothers out of their sleep in order to bid them—sleep on!

'Thou movest thyself, stretchest thyself, drawlest? Up! Up! Do not drawl—speak to me! Zarathustra the godless, calls thee!

'I, Zarathustra, the advocate of life, the advocate of suffering, the advocate of the circuit, I call thee, my most abysmal thought!

'Joy to me! Thou comest—I hear thee; my abyss *speaketh*; I have tilted my lowest depth into the light.

'Joy to me! Come hither! Give me thy hand —ha! Let alone! Aha!—Disgust, disgust, disgust—alas to me!'

Hardly had Zarathustra spoken these words when he fell down as one dead, and remained thus for a long time. When he came to himself again, however, he was pale and trembling; he did not get up, and for a long time declined to eat and drink. This condition continued for seven days; his animals, however, did not leave him day nor night, except that the eagle flew out to fetch food. And that which it fetched and foraged, it laid on

Zarathustra's couch, to such an extent that in the end he lay among red and yellow berries, grapes, rosy-cheeked apples, sweet-smelling herbage, and pine cones. At his feet, however, two lambs were stretched, which the eagle had with difficulty carried off from the shepherds.

At last, after seven days, Zarathustra sat up on his couch, took a rosy-cheeked apple in his hand, smelled it, and found its savour pleasant. Then his animals believed that the time was come to speak to him.

'O Zarathustra,' they said, 'thou hast lain thus for seven days with heavy eyes; wilt thou not get on thy feet once more?

'Step out of thy cave; the world waits for thee like a garden. The wind plays with strong fragrance which wants to reach thee, and all brooks would like to run after thee.

'All things long for thee, because thou hast remained alone for seven days; step out of thy cave! All things want to be thy physicians.

'Did perhaps a new knowledge come to thee, a bitter, grievous knowledge? Thou layest there like leavened dough, thy soul rose and swelled up over all its bounds.'—

'Oh, my animals,' answered Zarathustra, 'talk on thus, and let me listen! It refreshes me so much to hear you talk; where there is talk the world is as a garden to me.

'How good it is that there are words and tones; are not words and tones rainbows and seeming bridges between things eternally separated?

'To every soul belongs a different world, to every soul every other soul is a back-world.

'And it is among the most similar things that appearances deceive most delightfully, for the smallest gap is most difficult to bridge over.

'For me—how could there be aught external to me? There is no external! But we forget always on hearing tones; how good it is for us to forget!

'Are not names and sounds given to things, that man may reanimate himself therewith? It is a fine folly, speaking; man dances on everything with it.

'How good is all talk, and all the falsehood of sounds! With sounds one's love dances on many-hued rainbows.'

'O Zarathustra,' answered the animals, 'to those who think as we do, all things dance themselves: a thing comes and welcomes itself, and laughs and flees—and returns.

'Everything departs, everything returns; the wheel of existence rolls eternally. All dies, all revives again, the year of existence runs eternally.

'All disintegrates, all is integrated anew, the like house of existence builds itself eternally. All separates, all hails itself again; the ring of existence remains true to itself eternally.

'Every moment existence begins; round every "Here" rolls the sphere "There." The middle is everywhere. The path of eternity is crooked.'—

'Oh, ye roguish fools and barrel-organs,' answered Zarathustra, and smiled once more, 'how well ye know what had to be fulfilled in seven days;

'And how that monster crept into my throat and choked me! But I bit off its head and spat it away.

'And ye—ye had made a hurdy-gurdy ditty out of it? Now, however, I lie here, still exhausted with that biting and spitting away, still sick with my own salvation.

'*And ye observed it all?* Oh, my animals, are ye also cruel? Did ye wish to observe my great pain, as men do? Man, you know, is the cruellest animal.

'Hitherto he has enjoyed himself most in viewing tragedies, bull-fights, and crucifixions; and when he invented hell, behold, that was his heaven on earth.

'When the great man cries, the little man runs swiftly thither, and his tongue hangs out of his mouth for very wantonness. He, however, calls it his sympathy.

'The little man, especially the poet, how passionately he accuses life in words! Hear him, but do not fail to hear the delight in all his accusing!

'Such accusers of life—life vanquishes them with a wink of the eye. "Thou lovest me," says the insolent one; "wait a little, I have no time for thee yet."

'Man is the cruellest animal towards himself: in whatever calls itself "sinner" and "bearer of the cross" and "penitent," do not fail to mark the exquisite delight in complaining and accusing!

'And I myself—do I thereby want to be an accuser of man? Ah, my animals, that only have I learned hitherto, that to man his wickedest is necessary for his best—

'That what is most wicked in him is his best *power*, the hardest stone for the greatest creator, and that man must become better *and* more wicked.

'I was not fixed on *this* cross that I might know that man is wicked, but I cried, as no one has ever cried hitherto:

'"Ah, that his wickedest is so very small! Ah, that his best is so very small!"

'The great disgust for man—*it* had choked me and crept into my throat; and what the soothsayer had prognosticated: "All is indifferent, nothing is worth while, knowledge strangles one."

'A prolonged gloom hobbled on before me, a fatally weary, fatally intoxicated melancholy, speaking with yawning mouth:

'"Eternally he returns, the man of whom thou art weary, the petty man": so yawned my melancholy, and trailed its foot, and could not fall asleep.

'The earth of human beings became a cavern to me, its breast sunk in, everything living became human dust and bones and a mouldering past.

'My sighing sat on all human graves, and was unable any longer to rise; my sighing and questioning croaked and choked, and gnawed and wailed day and night:

'"Alas, man returns eternally! The petty man returns eternally!"—

'Once I saw both of them naked, the greatest man and the least man: all-too-similar to each other—all-too-human even the greatest man!

'All-too-little the greatest man!—That was my loathing of man! And the eternal second-coming also of the least man!—That was my loathing of all existence!

'Alas, disgust! Disgust! Disgust!'—Thus spake Zarathustra, and sighed and shuddered; for he remembered his sickness. His animals, however, would not allow him to say any more.

'Do not speak any more, thou convalescent!' said his animals, 'but go out where the world waits for thee like a garden.

'Go out to the roses, the bees, and the flocks of doves! But especially to the singing-birds, to learn *singing* of them!

'Singing, you know, is for the convalescent; he who is well may talk. And if he who is well also wants songs, he wants other songs than the convalescent.'—

'Oh, ye roguish knaves and barrel-organs, do be silent!' answered Zarathustra, and smiled at his animals. 'How well ye know what consolation I devised for myself in seven days!

'To have to sing once more—I devised *that* consolation for myself and *this* convalescence. Are ye going to make a hurdy-gurdy ditty of that also?'—

'Do not talk further,' his animals answered once more; 'rather, thou convalescent, first get a lyre ready for thyself, a new lyre.

'For, behold, O Zarathustra, new lyres are needed for new songs.

'Sing and bubble over, O Zarathustra, heal thy soul with new songs, that thou mayest bear thy great fate, which has not yet been the fate of any one!

'For thy animals know well, O Zarathustra, who thou art and must become: behold, *thou art the teacher of the eternal second coming*—that is now *thy* fate!

'That thou must be the first to teach this doctrine—how could this great fate fail to be thy greatest danger and infirmity!

'Behold, we know what thou teachest: that all things return eternally and we ourselves with them, and that we have already existed times without number and all things with us.

'Thou teachest that there is a great year of Becoming, an immensely great year, which, like a sandglass, must ever turn anew, to run down and run out anew:

'So that all these years are like one another in big and in little; so that we ourselves in every great year are like ourselves in big and in little.

'And if thou wantedst to die at present, O Zarathustra, behold, we know also how thou wouldst talk to thyself then; but thy animals beseech thee not to die yet!

'Thou wouldst speak without trembling, buoyant rather with bliss, for a great weight and oppression would be taken from thee, thou who art most patient!—

'"Now I die and disappear," thou wouldst say, "and in a moment I shall be nothing. Souls are as mortal as bodies.

'"But the plexus of causes returns in which I am interlaced; it will create me again! I myself belong to the causes of the eternal second coming.

'"I come again with this sun, with this earth, with this eagle, with this serpent—*not* to a new life, or a better life, or a similar life;

'"I come again eternally to this identical life, this self-same life in big and in little, to teach again the eternal second coming of all things—

'"To speak again the word of the great noonday of earth and man, to make known the overman once more to the human race.

'"I have spoken my word, I perish by my word: so my eternal fate decrees—as prophet I succumb!

'"The hour has now come for the departing one to bless himself. Thus—*ends* Zarathustra's departure."'

When the animals had spoken these words they were silent, and waited so that Zarathustra might say something to them; but Zarathustra did not hear that they were silent. On the contrary, he lay still with his eyes shut, like a person sleeping, although he did not sleep; for he communed just then with his soul. The serpent, however, and the eagle, when they found him silent in this manner, respected the great quiet around him and prudently withdrew.

THUS SPAKE ZARATHUSTRA, IV.

ZARATHUSTRA AND THE HIGHER MEN.

It was late in the afternoon only when Zarathustra, after long, useless searching and strolling, again returned home to his cave. When he stood opposite to it, however, at a distance of less than twenty paces, the thing happened which he now least of all expected: he heard anew the great *cry of distress*. And strange! this time the cry came out of his own cave! It was, however, a long, manifold, peculiar cry, and Zarathustra plainly distinguished that it was composed of many voices, although, heard at a distance, it might sound like the cry out of a single mouth.

Thereupon Zarathustra ran up to his cave, and behold! what a spectacle awaited him after that vocal performance! For there they all sat collected together whom he had met during the day: the king on the right, and the king on the left, the old magician, the pope, the voluntary beggar, the shadow, the intellectually scrupulous one, the sorrowful soothsayer, and the ass; the unsightliest man, however, had set a crown on his head, and had put round him two purple girdles; for like all the unsightly, he liked to disguise himself and play the handsome person. In the midst of that sorrowful company stood the eagle of Zarathustra, ruffled and disquieted, for it had been called on to answer too much, for which its pride had not any answer; the wise serpent, however, hung round its neck.

Zarathustra viewed all this with great astonishment; he then scrutinised each of his guests with courteous curiosity, read their souls, and wondered anew. In the meantime the assembled ones had risen from their seats, and waited with reverence in order that Zarathustra might speak. And Zarathustra spake thus:—

'Ye despairing ones! Ye strange ones! So it was *your* cry of distress I heard? And now I know where he is to be sought, whom I have vainly sought to-day: *the higher man.*

'He sits in my own cave, the higher man! But why do I wonder! Have I not myself allured him to me by honey offerings, and artful, luring calls of my happiness?

'But it seems to me ye are badly suited for company: ye make each other's hearts peevish, ye, who call for help when ye sit here together? Some one must first come—

'Some one who will make you laugh once more, a good jovial buffoon, a dancer, a wind, a wild romp, some old fool; what think ye?

'Forgive me, however, ye despairing ones, for speaking such trivial words before you, unworthy, verily, of such guests! But ye do not divine what makes my heart wanton.

'Ye yourselves do so, and your aspect: forgive it me! Every one, you know, becomes courageous at the sight of those in despair. To speak comfort to the despairing—every one thinks himself strong enough for it.

'To me ye have given this power—a good gift, my honourable guests! Well, do not then be angry when I also offer you something of my own.

'This is my empire and domain; that which is mine, however, shall be yours this evening and to-night. My animals shall serve you; let my cave be your resting-place!

'At house and home with me no one shall despair; in my purlieus I protect every one from the wild animals. And that is the first thing I offer you: security!

'The second thing, however, which I offer, is my little finger. And when ye have got *it*, take just the whole hand; yea, and the heart also! Welcome here, welcome to you, my guests!'

Thus spake Zarathustra, and laughed with love and wantonness. After this greeting the guests bowed once more and remained reverentially silent; the king on the right, however, answered him thus in their name:—

'O Zarathustra, by the manner in which thou hast given us thy hand and thy greeting, we know thee to be Zarathustra. Thou hast humbled thyself before us; thou hast almost hurt our reverence.

'Who, however, could have humbled himself as thou hast done, with so much pride? *That* revives us ourselves; it is a refreshment to our eyes and hearts.

'To behold it merely, we would gladly have ascended higher mountains than this. We have come, you know, as persons eager to behold; we wanted to see what brightened sorrowful eyes.

'And lo! it is now all over with our cries of distress. Our minds and hearts now stand open and are enraptured. Little is lacking for our spirits to become wanton.

'O Zarathustra, there is nothing grows more pleasingly on earth than a grand, strong will—it is the earth's finest growth. An entire landscape regales itself on one such tree.

'It is to the pine, O Zarathustra, that I compare him who grows up like thee—tall, silent, hardy, alone, of the most flexible material, stately;

'In the end, however, grasping out for a domain with strong, green boughs, asking weighty questions of the wind and the storm, and of whatever is indigenous in high places;

'Answering more weightily, a commander, a victor. Oh, who would not ascend high mountains to see such growths?

'From thy tree here, O Zarathustra, the mournful and the unfortunate also refresh themselves; at thy look even the wavering become steady and heal their hearts.

'And verily, to thy mountain and thy tree many eyes turn at the present day; a great longing has arisen, and many have learned to ask: "Who is Zarathustra?"

'And those into whose ears thou hast at any time dripped thy song and thy honey—all the hidden ones, the lone-dwellers and the twain-dwellers—have simultaneously said in their hearts:

'"Does Zarathustra still live? It is no longer worth our while to live; to us everything is indifferent, everything is useless, or—we must live with Zarathustra!

'"Why does he not come who has so long announced himself?"—thus does many a one ask. "Has solitude swallowed him up? Or should we perhaps go to him?"

'And that we despairing ones have just come into thy cave, and now no longer despair—that is but a prognostic and a presage that better ones are on the way to thee.

'For they themselves are on the way to thee, the last remnant of God among men—that is to say, all the men of great longing, of great loathing, of great satiety—

'All who do not want to live unless they learn again to *hope*—unless they learn from thee, O Zarathustra, the *great* hope!'

Thus spake the king on the right, and seized the hand of Zarathustra in order to kiss it. But Zarathustra checked his veneration and stepped back frightened, fleeing, as it were, silently and suddenly into the far distance. After a brief space, however, he was again at home with his guests, and gazing upon them with clear scrutinising eyes, he said:—

'My guests, ye higher men, I will speak plain language and plainly with you. It is not for you that I have waited here in these mountains.'

('"Plain language and plainly?" Good God!' said the king on the left to himself; 'one sees he does not know the good occidentals, this sage out of the orient!

'But he means "blunt language and plainly" —well! that is not the worst taste in these days.')

'Ye may verily, all of you, be higher men,' continued Zarathustra; 'but for me ye are neither high enough nor strong enough.

'For me, that is, for the inexorable which is now silent in me, but will not always be silent. And if ye appertain to me, still it is not as my right arm.

'For, sure enough, all who, like you, have infirm and tender limbs, want above all things to be *treated indulgently,* whether they are conscious thereof, or hide it from themselves.

'I do not, however, treat my arms and legs indulgently; *I do not treat my warriors indulgently.* How then could ye be fit for my warfare?

'With you I should spoil all my victories. And many of you would even tumble down, if ye merely heard the loud beating of my drums.

'Moreover, ye are not sufficiently handsome and well-born for me. I require pure smooth mirrors for my doctrines; my own likeness is still distorted on your surface.

'Many a burden presses on your shoulders, many a recollection, many a mischievous dwarf squats on your corners. In you, also, there are concealed traits of the populace.

'And although ye are high and of a higher type, much in you is crooked and misshapen; there is no smith in the world who could hammer you right and straight for me.

'Ye are merely bridges; may higher ones pass over on you! Ye signify steps; so do not be angry with him who ascends to *his* height above you!

'Out of your seed there may one day arise a true son and a perfect heir for me; but that is far off. Ye yourselves are not those to whom my heritage and my name belong.

'It is not for you that I wait here in these mountains; it is not with you that I can descend for the last time. Ye have come only as a presage that higher ones are on the way to me.—

'Not the men of great longing, of great loathing, of great satiety, nor what ye call the last remnant of God.

'Nay! Nay! Thrice Nay! It is for *others* that I wait here in these mountains, and will not lift my foot hence without them—

'For higher men, stronger men, more triumphant men, merrier men, such men as are squarely built in body and soul; *laughing lions* must come!

'Oh, my guests, ye strange ones—have ye not heard anything of my children? And that they are on the way to me?

'Do speak to me of my garden, of my Happy Isles, of my new, beautiful race—why do ye not speak to me thereof?

'I solicit it as a guest's bounty, from your love, that ye speak to me of my children. For their sake I am rich, for their sake I became poor; what have I not surrendered?—

'What would I not surrender that I might have one thing: *those* children, *that* living plantation, *those* life-trees of my will and my highest hope!'

Thus spake Zarathustra, and stopped suddenly in his talk, for his longing came upon him. And all his guests also were silent and stood still, astounded, only the old soothsayer made signs with his hands and his countenance.

Made in the USA
Columbia, SC
10 January 2023

10000236R00167